German

English edition prepared by First Edition Translations Ltd,
Great Britain
Designed and produced by AA Publishing
First published in 1995 as Wat & Hoe Portugees,
© Uitgeverij Kosmos bv - Utrecht/Antwerpen
Van Dale Lexicografie bv - Utrecht/Antwerpen
This edition © Automobile Association Developments Limited 2005

A CIP catalogue record for this book is available from the
British Library
Published by AA Publishing (a trading name of Automobile
Association Developments Limited, whose registered office is
Fanum House, Basingstoke, Hampshire RG21 4EA.
Registered number 1878835)

A02536

Typeset by Information Engineers, Cambridge.
Printed and bound by Everbest Printing Co Ltd, China.
Find out more about AA Publishing and the wide range of services
the AA provides by visiting our web site at
www.theAA.com/bookshop

Contents

Introduction

● **Welcome to the AA's essential Phrase Books series,** covering the most popular European languages and containing everything you'd expect from a comprehensive language series. They're concise, accessible and easy to understand, and you'll find them indispensable on your trip abroad.

Each guide is divided into 15 themed sections and starts with a pronunciation table which gives you the phonetic spelling to all the words and phrases you'll need to know for your trip, while at the back of the book is an extensive word list and grammar guide which will help you construct basic sentences in your chosen language.

Throughout the book you'll come across coloured boxes with a 👉 beside them. These are designed to help you if you can't understand what your listener is saying to you. Hand the book over to them and encourage them to point to the appropriate answer to the question you are asking.

Other coloured boxes in the book – this time without the symbol – give alphabetical listings of themed words with their English translations beside them.

For extra clarity, we have put all English words and phrases in black, foreign language terms in brown and their phonetic pronunciation in italic.

This phrase book covers all subjects you are likely to come across during the course of your visit, from reserving a room for the night to ordering food and drink at a restaurant and what to do if your car breaks down or you lose your traveller's cheques and money. With over 2,000 commonly used words and essential phrases at your fingertips you can rest assured that you will be able to get by in all situations, so let the essential Phrase Book become your passport to a secure and enjoyable trip!

Pronunciation table

The pronunciation provided should be read as if it were English, bearing in mind the following main points:

Vowels

a	is like **ar**	ar	as in **Kater**	karter
	or the **u** in cup	u	as in **Tasse**	tusser
ä	is like **ay** in may	ay	as in **spät**	shpayt
	or **e** in edible	e	as in **hält**	helt
e	is like **ay** in may	ay	as in **Nebel**	naybel
	or **e** in edible	e	as in **Mensch**	mensh
	or **air** in fair	air	as in **Schmerz**	shmairts
i	is like **i** in lick	i	as in **Mitte**	mitter
o	is like **oa** in boat	oa	as in **Motor**	moator
	or **o** in lock	o	as in **Socke**	zokker
ö	is like **u** in fur	oe	as in **öffnen**	oefnen
u	is like **oo** in ooze	oo	as in **Kur**	koor
ü	is like **ue** in cue	ue	as in **fünf**	fuenf

Consonants

Consonants are mainly as in English except for

g	like **g** in great	g	as in **Gigant**	gigant
j	like **y** in yes	y	as in **ja**	yar
s	when at beginning of word, like **z**	z	as in **Seife**	zaifer
v	like **f** in fish	f	as in **Volk**	folk
w	like **v** in vole	v	as in **Wagen**	vargen
z	like **ts** in cats	ts	as in **zwölf**	tsvoelf

At the end of a word **b**, **d**, and **g** change in sound to **p**, **t** and **k** respectively. The symbol **ß** (es-tset) stands for **ss** and is rare.

Some combinations of letters

au is pronounced *ow* as in cow; **eu** and **äu** are pronounced *oy* as in boy; **ie** is pronounced *ee* as in feet; **ei** and **ai** are pronounced as *ai* in Thai; **ch** is like **ch** in loch but rendered in the pronunciation as *kh*; **qu** is pronounced *kv*; **sp** and **st** at the start of a word are pronounced *shp* and *sht*; **sch** is also pronounced **sh**.

Stress

Usually on the leading syllable or on the stem (root) of the word, e.g. **stehen** (to stand) is stressed *shtayen*, **verstehen** (to understand) is stressed *fairshtayen*.

1

Useful lists

1.1 Today or tomorrow?

What day is it today?	Welcher Tag ist heute?	
	velkher tark ist hoyter?	
Today's Monday	Heute ist Montag	
	hoyter ist moantark	
– Tuesday	Heute ist Dienstag	
	hoyter ist deenstark	
– Wednesday	Heute ist Mittwoch	
	hoyter ist mittvokh	
– Thursday	Heute ist Donnerstag	
	hoyter ist donnerstark	
– Friday	Heute ist Freitag	
	hoyter ist fraitark	
– Saturday	Heute ist Samstag/Sonnabend (S. Germany/ N. Germany)	
	hoyter ist zamstark/zonnarbent	
– Sunday	Heute ist Sonntag	
	hoyter ist zonntark	
in January	im Januar	
	im yannooar	
since February	seit Februar	
	zait frebrooar	
in spring	im Frühling	
	im fruehling	
in summer	im Sommer	
	im zommer	
in autumn	im Herbst	
	im hairpst	
in winter	im Winter	
	im vinter	
1997	neunzehnhundertsiebenundneunzig	
	noyntsayn hoondert zeeben oont noyntsikh	
the twentieth century	das zwanzigste Jahrhundert	
	dass tsvantsikhster yarhoondert	

What's the date today?	**Der wievielte ist heute?**
	dayr veefeelter ist hoyter?
Today's the 24th	**Heute ist der vierundzwanzigste**
	hoyter ist dayr fear oont tsvantsikhster
Monday 3 November 1998	**Montag, der 3 November 1998**
	moantark dayr dritter november noyntsayn hoondert akht oont noyntsikh
in the morning	**morgens**
	morgens
midday	**mittags** (from about 11.30–2pm)
	mittarks
in the afternoon	**nachmittags**
	nakhmittarks
in the evening	**abends**
	arbents
at night	**nachts**
	nakhts
this morning	**heute morgen**
	hoyter morgen
this afternoon	**heute mittag**
	hoyter mittark
this evening	**heute nachmittag**
	hoyter nakhmittark
tonight	**heute abend**
	hoyter arbent
last night	**letzte nacht**
	letster nakht
this week	**diese Woche**
	deezer vokher
next month	**nächsten Monat**
	nexten moanart
last year	**voriges Jahr**
	forigez yar
next...	**nächste(n)/nächstes...**
	nexter(n)/nextes
in...days/weeks/ months/years	**in ... Tagen/Wochen/Monaten/Jahren**
	in ... targen/vokhen/moanarten/yaren

...weeks ago	vor ... Wochen
	for ... vokhen
day off	der freie Tag
	dayr fraier tark

1.2 Bank holidays

● **The most important** bank holidays in Germany are the following:

January 1	New Year's Day (Neujahr)
January 6	Epiphany (Hl. Drei Könige)
March/April	Good Friday, Easter and Easter Monday
	(Karfreitag, Ostersonntag und Ostermontag
May 1	May Day (Maifeiertag)
May	Ascension Day (Christi Himmelfahrt)
May/June	Whit Sunday and Whit Monday
	(Pfingstsonntag und Pfingstmontag)
*June	Corpus Christi (Fronleichnam)
*August 15	Feast of the Assumption (Mariä Himmelfahrt)
October 3	Day of German Unity (Tag der deutschen Einheit)
*November 1	All Saint's Day (Allerheiligen)
*November (Wed, variable)	Buss- und Bettag (day to repent and pray)
December 25/26	Christmas (Weihnachten)

Most shops, banks and government institutions are closed on these days. The dates marked with an asterisk are Catholic holidays and are mainly celebrated in the south of Germany. On Christmas Eve banks and shops tend to be closed in the afternoon.

1.3 What time is it?

What time is it? _____	Wie spät ist es?
	vee shpayt ist ez?
It's nine o'clock _____	Es ist neun Uhr
	ez ist noyn ooer
- five past ten _____	Es ist fünf nach zehn
	ez ist fuenf nakh tsayn
- a quarter past eleven _	Es ist Viertel nach elf
	ez ist feartel nakh elf
- twenty past twelve ___	Es ist zehn nach zwölf
	ez ist tsayn nakh tsvoelf
- half past one _____	Es ist halb zwei
	ez ist halp tsvai
- twenty–five to three _	Es ist fünf nach halb drei
	ez ist fuenf nakh halp drai
- a quarter to four _____	Es ist Viertel vor vier
	ez ist feartel for fear
- ten to five _____	Es ist zehn vor fünf
	ez ist tsayn for fuenf
- twelve noon _____	Es ist zwölf
	ez ist tsvoelf
- midnight _____	Es ist Mitternacht
	ez ist mitternakht
half an hour _____	eine halbe Stunde
	ainer halber shtoonder
What time? _____	Um wieviel Uhr?
	oom veefeel ooer?
What time can I come _ round?	Wann kann ich vorbeikommen?
	vann kann ikh for bai kommen?
At... _____	Um...*oom...*
After... _____	Nach...*nakh...*
Before... _____	Vor...*for...*
Between...and... _____	Zwischen... und...
	tsvishen ... oont...

From...to... _____	Von ... bis...
	fon ... biss...
In...minutes _____	In ... Minuten
	in ... meenooten
– an hour _____	In einer Stunde
	in ainer shtoonder
– ...hours _____	In... Stunden
	In... shtoonden
– a quarter of an hour __	In einer Viertelstunde
	in ainer feartel shtoonder
– three quarters of _____ an hour	In einer Dreiviertelstunde
	in ainer drai feartel shtoonder
early/late _____	zu früh/spät
	tsoo frue/shpayt
on time _____	rechtzeitig
	rekht tsaitikh
summertime _____	(die) Sommerzeit
	(dee) zommer tsait
wintertime _____	(die) Winterzeit
	(dee) vinter tsait

1.4 One, two, three...

0 _____	null *nooll*
1 _____	eins *ains*
2 _____	zwei *tsvai*
3 _____	drei *drai*
4 _____	vier *fear*
5 _____	fünf *fuenf*
6 _____	sechs *zekhs*
7 _____	sieben *zeeben*
8 _____	acht *akht*
9 _____	neun *noyn*
10 _____	zehn *tsayn*

11	_____	elf	*elf*
12	_____	zwölf	*tsvoelf*
13	_____	dreizehn	*draitsayn*
14	_____	vierzehn	*feartsayn*
15	_____	fünfzehn	*fuenftsayn*
16	_____	sechzehn	*zekhtsayn*
17	_____	siebzehn	*zeeptsayn*
18	_____	achtzehn	*akht-tsayn*
19	_____	neunzehn	*noyntsayn*
20	_____	zwanzig	*tsvantsikh*
21	_____	einundzwanzig	*ain oont tsvantsikh*
22	_____	zweiundzwanzig	*tsvai oont tsvantsikh*
30	_____	dreissig	*draissikh*
31	_____	einunddreissig	*ain oont draissikh*
32	_____	zweiunddreissig	*tsvai oont draissikh*
40	_____	vierzig	*feartsikh*
50	_____	fünfzig	*fuenftsikh*
60	_____	sechzig	*zekhtsikh*
70	_____	siebzig	*zeeptsikh*
80	_____	achtzig	*akhttsikh*
90	_____	neunzig	*noyntsikh*
100	_____	hundert	*hoondert*
101	_____	hunderteins	*hoondert ains*
110	_____	hundertzehn	*hoondert tsayn*
120	_____	hundertzwanzig	*hoondert tsvantsikh*
200	_____	zweihundert	*tsvai hoondert*
300	_____	dreihundert	*drai hoondert*
400	_____	vierhundert	*fear hoondert*
500	_____	fünfhundert	*fuenf hoondert*
600	_____	sechshundert	*zekhs hoondert*
700	_____	siebenhundert	*zeeben hoondert*
800	_____	achthundert	*akht hoondert*
900	_____	neunhundert	*noyn hoondert*
1,000	_____	tausend	*towzent*

1,100	_____	tausendeinhundert *towzent ain hoondert*
2,000	_____	zweitausend *tsvai towzent*
10,000	_____	zehntausend *tsayn towzent*
100,000	_____	hunderttausend *hoondert towzent*
1,000,000	_____	eine Million *ainer millioan*
1st	_____	erste *erster*
2nd	_____	zweite *tsvaiter*
3rd	_____	dritte *dritter*
4th	_____	vierte *fearter*
5th	_____	fünfte *fuenfter*
6th	_____	sechste *zekhster*
7th	_____	sieb(en)te *zeeb(en)ter*
8th	_____	achte *akhter*
9th	_____	neunte *noynter*
10th	_____	zehnte *tsaynter*
11th	_____	elfte *elfter*
12th	_____	zwölfte *tsvoelfter*
13th	_____	dreizehnter *draitsaynter*
14th	_____	vierzehnte *feartsaynter*
15th	_____	fünfzehnte *fuenftsaynter*
16th	_____	sechzehnte *zekhtsaynter*
17th	_____	siebzehnte *zeeptsaynter*
18th	_____	achtzehnte *akht-tsaynter*
19th	_____	neunzehnte *noyntsaynter*
20th	_____	zwanzigste *tsvantsikhster*
21st	_____	einundzwanzigste *ain oont tsvantsikhster*
22nd	_____	zweiundzwanzigste *tsvai oont tsvantsikhster*
30th	_____	dreissigste *draissikhster*
100th	_____	hundertste *hoondertster*
1,000th	_____	tausendste *towzentster*
once	_____	einmal *ainmarl*
twice	_____	zweimal *tsvaimarl*
double	_____	das Doppelte *dass doppelter*

triple _____	das Dreifache *dass draifakher*
half _____	die Hälfte *dee haelfter*
a quarter _____	ein Viertel *ain feartel*
a third _____	ein Drittel *ain dritel*
a couple, a few, some __	ein paar, einige, mehrere *ain par, ainiger, mayrerer*

2+4=6 _____	zwei und vier ist sechs *tsvai oont fear ist zekhs*
4-2=2 _____	vier weniger zwei ist zwei *fear vayniger tsvai ist tsvai*
2x4=8 _____	zwei mal vier ist acht *tsvai marl fear ist akht*
4÷2=2 _____	vier geteilt durch zwei ist zwei *fear getailt doorkh tsvai ist tsvai*

odd/even _____	gerade/ungerarde *gerarder/oongerader*
total _____	(ins)gesamt *(ins)gezammt*
6x9 _____	sechs mal neun *zekhs marl noyn*

1.5 The weather

Is the weather going to be good/bad?	Wird das Wetter schön/schlecht? *virt dass vetter shoen/shlekht?*
Is it going to get colder/hotter?	Wird es kälter/wärmer? *virt es kaelter/vaermer?*
What temperature is it going to be?	Wieviel Grad wird es? *veefeel grart virt ez?*
Is it going to rain?	Wird es regnen? *virt ez raygnen?*
Is there going to be a storm?	Bekommen wir Sturm? *bekommen veer shturm?*

Bewölkung	kalt	Rückenwind
cloud	cold	tail wind
Böen	klar	Schnee
squalls	clear	snow
frisch	kühl	schwül
chilly	chilly	muggy
(temperature),	leicht bewölkt	sehr heiss
fresh (wind)	cloudy	scorching hot
Frost	leichte Bewölkung	sonnig
frost	light clouds	sunny
Glatteis	mild	Sprühregen
black ice	mild	drizzle
... Grad (unter/über	nasskalt	stark bewölkt
Null)	cold and damp	overcast
... degrees	Nebel	starke Bewölkung
(above/below	fog	heavy clouds
zero)	Orkan	Sturm
Graupel/Hagel	hurricane	storm
hail	rauh	Wind (leichter/
heiter	bleak	mässiger/starker)
fine	Regenschauer	light/moderate/strong
heiss	shower	wind
hot	Regen(schauer)	windig
Hitzewelle	rain	windy
heat wave		

Is it going to snow? ____	Wird es schneien?
	virt es shnaien?
Is it going to freeze? ___	Wird es frieren?
	virt es freeren?
Is the thaw setting in?__	Wird es tauen?
	virt es towen?
Is it going to be foggy?_	Bekommen wir Nebel?
	bekommen veer naybel?
Is there going to be a __	Wird es ein Gewitter geben?
thunderstorm?	*virt es ain gevitter gayben?*

The weather's changing	Das Wetter schlägt um
	dass vetter shlaekt oom
It's cooling down _____	Es kühlt sich ab
	ez kuehlt zikh ap
What's the weather _____ going to be like today	Was für Wetter wird heute?
	vass fuer vetter virt hoyter?

1.6 Here, there...

See also 5.1 Asking for directions

here/there _____	hier/da
	heer/dar
somewhere/nowhere ___	irgendwo/nirgendwo
	eergentvoa/neergentvoa
everywhere _____	überall
	ueberall
far away/nearby _____	weit weg/in der Nähe
	vait vek/in dayr nayher
right/left _____	nach rechts/links
	nakh rekhts/links
to the right/left of _____	rechts/links von
	rekhts/links fon
straight ahead_____	geradeaus
	gerarder ows
via _____	über
	ueber
in _____	in
	in
on _____	auf
	owf
under _____	unter
	oonter
against _____	gegen
	gaygen

opposite	gegenüber
	gaygen ueber
next to	neben
	nayben
near	bei
	bai
in front of	vor
	for
in the centre	in der Mitte
	in dayr mitter
forward	nach vorn
	nakh forn
down	(nach) unten
	(nakh) oonten
up	(nach) oben
	(nakh) owben
inside	drinnen
	drinnen
outside	draussen/raus
	drowssen/rows
behind	(nach) hinten
	(nakh) hinten
at the front	vorn
	forn
at the back	hinten
	hinten
in the north	im Norden
	im norden
to the south	nach Süden
	nakh zueden
from the west	aus dem Westen
	ows dem vesten
from the east	aus dem Osten
	ows daym ossten
north, east, south, west of	nördlich/östlich/südlich/westlich von
	noerdlikh/oestlikh/zuedlikh/vestlikh fon

1.7 What does that sign say?

See also 5.4 Traffic signs

Abfahrt exit
Achtung beware
Ankunft
arrival
Aufzug lift
Ausgang
exit
Auskunft
information
Bahnhof
station
Bitte nicht stören
Do not disturb
Drücken
push
Durchgang
throughway
Eingang
entrance
Eintritt frei/verboten
free entry/no entry
Empfang
reception
Erste Hilfe
first aid
Fahrkarten
tickets
Fahrstuhl
lift
Freibad
open-air swimming-
  pool

Fremdenverkehrs-
  verein
tourist information
Fussgänger
pedestrians
Gasthaus/Gasthof
inn
Gefahr danger
Geöffnet open
Gepäckannahme/
  -aufbewahrung
check-in/left-luggage
Geschlossen
closed
Gleis
platform
Hausmeister
caretaker
Herein!
Come in!
Kein Trinkwasser
No drinking water
Nicht berühren!
Please do not touch!
Notausgang/-treppe
emergency exit/stairs
Öffnungszeiten
opening hours
Pförtner
porter
Polizei
police

Rathaus
town hall/city hall
Rauchen verboten
no smoking
Reserviert
reserved
Rundfahrt tour
Schliessfach
left luggage
  locker/safe deposit
  box
Schwimmbad
swimming-pool
Selbstbedienung
self-service
Stock floor
Treppe stairs
Vorsicht!
beware
Warnung
beware/warning
Warteraum/-saal
waiting room
Wechselstube
exchange office
Ziehen pull
Zimmer frei/zu
  vermieten
vacancy (room)/
room to let
Zugang
access/entry

1.8 Telephone alphabet

a	_ar_	wie Anton	_vee arnton_
ä	_ay_	wie Ärger	_vee airger_
b	_beh_	wie Berta	_vee berter_
c	_tseh_	wie Cäsar	_vee tsezer_
ch	_tseh-har_	wie Charlotte	_vee sharlotter_
d	_deh_	wie Dora	_vee doara_
e	_eh_	wie Emil	_vee aymil_
f	_ef_	wie Friedrich	_vee freedrikh_
g	_geh_	wie Gustav	_vee goostaf_
h	_hah_	wie Heinrich	_vee hainrikh_
i	_ee_	wie Ida	_vee eeda_
j	_yot_	wie Julius	_vee yoolius_
k	_kah_	wie Kaufmann	_vee kowfmann_
l	_el_	wie Ludwig	_vee loodvikh_
m	_em_	wie Martha	_vee marta_
n	_en_	wie Nordpol	_vee nortpole_
o	_oh_	wie Otto	_vee ottoa_
ö	_oe_	wie Ökonom	_vee oekonoam_
p	_peh_	wie Paula	_vee powla_
q	_koo_	wie Quelle	_vee kveller_
r	_air_	wie Richard	_vee rikhart_
sch	_es-tseh-har_	wie Schule	_vee shooler_
s	_es_	wie Samuel	_vee zarmooel_
t	_teh_	wie Theodor	_vee tayoador_
u	_oo_	wie Ulrich	_vee oolrikh_
ü	_ue_	wie Übermut	_vee uebermoot_
v	_fow_	wie Viktor	_vee viktor_
w	_veh_	wie Wilhelm	_vee vilhelm_
x	_iks_	wie Xanthippe	_vee ksantippeh_
y	_uepsilon_	wie Ypsilon	_vee uepsilon_
z	_tset_	wie Zacharias	_vee tsakharias_

1.9 Personal details

surname _____	(der) Nachname
	(dayr) nakhnarmer
christian name _____	(der) Vorname
	(dayr) fornarmer
initials _____	(der) Anfangsbuchstabe des Vornamens
	(dayr) an-fangs-bookh-shtarber dess
	fornarmenz
address (street/ _____	(die) Anschrift (Strasse/Nummer)
number)	*(dee) anshrift (shtrasser/noommer)*
post code/town _____	(die) Postleitzahl/(der) Wohnort
	(dee) posst-lait-tsarl/(dayr) voanort
sex (male/female) _____	(das) Geschlecht (m.= männlich,
	w.= weiblich)
	(dass) geschlekht (m.= maennlikh, w. =
	vaiblikh)
nationality _____	(die) Staatsangehörigkeit
	(dee) shtarts-ange-hoerikh-kait
date of birth_____	(das) Geburtsdatum
	(dass) geboorts dartum
place of birth_____	(der) Geburtsort
	(dayr) geboorts ort
occupation _____	(der) Beruf *(dayr) beroof*
married/single/ _____	verheiratet/ledig/geschieden
divorced	*fairhai-rartet/laydikh/gescheeden*
widowed _____	(die) Witwe/(der) Witwer
	(dee) vitveh/ (dayr) vitver
(number of) children____	(Zahl der) Kinder
	(tsarl dayr) kinder
identity card/passport/ _	Personalausweis/Reisepass/Führerschein
driving licence number	- nummer,
	pair zoanarl owsvaiz-
	raizerparss/fuerershain-nummer
place and date of _____	Ort und Datum der Ausstellung
issue	*ort oont dartoom dayr owsshtelloong*

2 Courtesies

● **It is usual in Germany** to shake hands on meeting and parting company.

2.1 Greetings

● **The correct pronoun** to use in formal greetings is '*Sie*' (zee) – which translates as 'you' – in the singular and plural. '*Sie*' should be employed when addressing people over the age of 18 except when talking to intimates. Conversation within the family, or between children, youths, students, friends and close work colleagues requires the use of the familiar second person pronoun '*du*' (doo). Please note that among adults it is usual for the older person to offer the more familiar address of '*du*' to the younger one.

Hello, Mr... _____	Guten Tag, Herr...
	gooten tark, hair...
Hello, Mrs... _____	Guten Tag, Frau...
	gooten tark, frow...
Hello, Peter _____	Hallo, Peter
	hallo, payter
Hi, Helen _____	Tag, Helene
	tark, helayner
Good morning _____	Guten Morgen
	gooten morgen
Good afternoon _____	Guten Tag
	gooten tark
Good evening _____	Guten Abend
	gooten arbent
How are you? _____	Wie geht's?
	vee gayts?
Fine, thank you, and ___ you?	Sehr gut, und Ihnen?
	zayr goot, oont eenen?
Very well_____	Ausgezeichnet
	ows ge tsaikh net
Not very well _____	Nicht besonders
	nikht bezonderz

Not too bad _____	Es geht
	ez gayt
I'd better be going ____	Dann geh' ich mal
	dann gay' ikh mall
I have to be going.____ Someone's waiting for me	Ich muss los. Ich werde erwartet *ikh mooss loas. ikh verder ervartet*
Bye!_____	Tschüs
	tshuess
Goodbye _____	Auf Wiedersehen
	owf veederzayn
See you soon _____	Bis bald
	biss balt
See you later_____	Bis gleich
	biss glaich
See you in a little while _	Bis dann
	biss dann
Sleep well _____	Schlafen Sie gut
	shlarfen zee goot
Good night _____	Gute Nacht
	gooter nakht
All the best _____	Alles Gute
	alles gooter
Have fun _____	Viel Vergnügen
	feel fairgnuegen
Good luck _____	Viel Glück
	feel gluek
Have a nice holiday ___	(Einen) schönen Urlaub
	(ainen) shoenen oorlowp
Have a good trip ____	Gute Reise
	gooter raizer
Thank you, you too ___	Danke, gleichfalls
	danker, glaikhfalz
Say hello to...for me ___	Schöne Grüsse an...
	shoener gruesser an...

2.2 How to ask a question

Who? _____	Wer?
	vayr?
Who's that? _____	Wer ist das?
	vayr ist dass?
What? _____	Was?
	vass?
What's there to _____ see here?	Was gibt es hier zu sehen?
	vass gipt ez heer tsoo zayhen?
What kind of hotel _____ is that?	Was für eine Art Hotel ist das?
	vass fuer ainer art hotel ist dass?
Where? _____	Wo?
	voe?
Where's the toilet? _____	Wo ist die Toilette?
	voe ist dee twaletter?
Where are you going? __	Wohin gehen/(by car) fahren Sie?
	vohin gayhen/fahren zee?
Where are you from? ___	Woher kommen Sie?
	vohair kommen zee?
How? _____	Wie?
	vee?
How far is that? _____	Wie weit ist das?
	vee vait ist dass?
How long does that ___ take?	Wie lange dauert das?
	vee langer dowert dass?
How long is the trip? ___	Wie lange dauert die Reise?
	vee langer dowert dee raizer?
How much? _____	Wieviel?
	veefeel?
How much is this? _____	Wieviel kostet das?
	veefeel kostet dass?
What time is it? _____	Wie spät ist es?
	vee shpayt ist ez?

Which? _____	Welcher (masculine), welches (neuter), welche (feminine, plural)
	velkher? velkherz? velkher?
Which glass is mine? __	Welches Glas ist für mich?
	velkherz glars ist fuer mikh?
When? _____	Wann?
	vann?
When are you leaving? _	Wann reisen Sie ab?
	vann raizen zee ap?
Why? _____	Warum?
	vahroom?
Could you...me?_____	Können Sie mir/mich...
	koennen zee meer/mikh...
Could you help me, ____ please?	Könnten Sie mir bitte helfen?
	koennten zee meer bitter helfen?
Could you point that __ out to me?	Können Sie mir das zeigen?
	koennen zee meer dass tsaygen?
Could you come_____ with me, please?	Würden Sie bitte mit mir mitgehen?
	vuerden zee bitter mit meer mitgayhen?
Could you..._____	Würden Sie bitte...?
	vuerden zee bitter...?
Could you reserve _____ some tickets for me, please?	Würden Sie bitte Karten für mich reservieren?
	vuerden zee bitter karten fuer mikh rezerveeren?
Do you know...? _____	Wissen Sie...?
	vissen zee...?
Do you know another __ hotel, please?	Könnten Sie mir ein anderes Hotel empfehlen?
	koennten zee meer ain anderez hotel empfaylen?
Do you know _____ whether...?	Wissen Sie ob..
	vissen zee op...
Do you have a...?_____	Haben Sie ein(en)/eine...?
	harben zee ain(en)/ainer...?

Do you have a _____ Haben Sie bitte ein vegetarisches
vegetarian dish, Gericht?
please? *harben zee bitter ain vegetarishers
gerikht?*

I'd like... _____ Ich möchte gern ...
ikh moekhter gayrn ...

I'd like a kilo of apples, _ Ich möchte bitte ein Kilo Äpfel
please. *ikh moekhter bitter ain kilo epfel*

Can I...? _____ Darf ich...?
darf ikh...?

Can I take this? _____ Darf ich dies mitnehmen?
darf ikh dees mittnaymen?

Can I smoke here?_____ Darf ich hier rauchen?
darf ikh heer rowkhen?

Could I ask you _____ Darf ich Sie etwas fragen?
something? *darf ikh zee etvass frargen?*

2.3 How to reply

Yes, of course_____ Ja, natürlich
yar, natuerlikh

No, I'm sorry _____ Nein, es tut mir leid
Nain, ez toot meer lait

Yes, what can I do _____ Ja, was kann ich für Sie tun?
for you? *yar, vass kann ikh fuer zee toon?*

Just a moment, please _ Einen Augenblick bitte
ainen owgen blick bitter

No, I don't have _____ Nein, ich habe jetzt keine Zeit
time now *nain, ikh haber yetst kainer tsait*

No, that's impossible___ Nein, das ist unmöglich
nain, dass ist oonmoeglikh

I think so _____ Ich glaube schon
ikh glowber shoan

I agree _____ Ich glaube (es) auch
ikh glowber (ez) owkh

I hope so too _____	Ich hoffe (es) auch
	ikh hoffer (ez) owkh
No, not at all _____	Nein, überhaupt nicht
	nain, ueberhowpt nikht
No, no-one _____	Nein, niemand
	nain, neemant
No, nothing _____	Nein, nichts
	nain, nikhts
That's (not) right _____	Das stimmt (nicht)
	dass shtimmt (nikht)
I (don't) agree _____	Da stimme ich Ihnen (nicht) zu
	dar shtimmer ikh eenen (nikht) tsoo
Okay _____	Einverstanden
	ain-fair-shtanden
Perhaps _____	vielleicht
	feelaikht
I don't know _____	Ich weiss es nicht
	ikh vaiss es nikht

2.4 Thank you

Thank you _____	Vielen Dank
	feelen dunk
You're welcome _____	Keine Ursache/gern geschehen
	kainer oorzakher/gayrn geshayhen
Thank you very much __	Vielen herzlichen Dank
	feelen hairtslikhen dunk
Very kind of you _____	Sehr freundlich (von Ihnen)
	zayr froyntlikh (fon eenen)
I enjoyed it very much__	Es war mir ein Vergnügen
	es var meer ain fairgnuegen
Thank you for your_____	Ich danke Ihnen für die Mühe
trouble	*ikh dunker eenen fuer dee muer*

You shouldn't have _____ Das wäre nicht nötig gewesen
dass vayrer nikht noetikh gevayzen

That's all right _____ Ist schon in Ordnung
ist shoan in ordnoong

2.5 Sorry

Excuse me _____ Verzeihung
fair tsaioong

Sorry! _____ Entschuldigung
ent shool digoong

I'm sorry, I didn't Entschuldigung, ich wusste nicht, dass...
know... _____ *ent shool digung, ikh vuster nihkt dass...*

I do apologise _____ Ich bitte vielmals um Verzeihung
ikh bitter feelmarls oom fair tsaioong

Please don't hold _____ Nehmen Sie (es) mir bitte nicht übel
it against me *naymen zee (es) meer bitter nikht uebel*

I'm sorry _____ Es tut mir leid
ez toot meer lait

I didn't do it on _____ Ich habe es nicht mit Absicht getan, es
purpose, it was an war ein Versehen
accident *ikh harber ez nikht mit apsikht getarn, ez
var ain fairzayhen*

That's all right _____ Das macht nichts
dass makht nikhts

Never mind _____ Lassen Sie nur
lassen zee noor

It could've happened _ Das kann jedem mal passieren
to anyone *dass kann yaydem marl passeeren*

31

2.6 What do you think?

Which do you prefer? __	Was ist Ihnen lieber?
	vass ist eenen leeber?
What do you think? ____	Was halten Sie davon?
	vass harlten zee dafonn?
I don't mind_____	Es ist mir egal
	ez ist meer egarl
Well done! _____	Sehr gut!
	zayr goot!
Not bad!_____	Nicht schlecht!
	nikht shlekht!
Great! _____	Ausgezeichnet!
	ows ge tsaykh net!
It's really nice here! ____	Hier ist es aber gemütlich!
	heer ist ez arber gemuetlikh!
How nice for you!_____	Wie hübsch/schön (für Sie/dich)!
	vee huepsh/shoen (fuer zee/dikh)!
I'm (not) very happy____ with...	Ich bin (nicht) sehr zufrieden über...
	ikh bin (nikht) zayr tsoofreeden ueber...
I'm glad..._____	Ich bin froh, dass...
	ikh bin froa, dass...
I'm having a great time _	Ich amüsiere mich sehr gut
	ikh amuezeerer mikh zayr goot
I'm looking forward to it	Ich freue mich drauf
	ikh froyer mikh drowf
Impossible _____	Unmöglich!
	oonmoeglikh!
That's terrible! _____	Wie scheußlich!
	vee shoysslikh!
What a pity!_____	Wie schade!
	vee sharder!
That's filthy! _____	Wie schmutzig/dreckig!
	vee shmootsikh/drekkikh!
What a load of rubbish!	(So'n) Quatsch!
	(zoan) kvatsh!

I don't like... _____ Ich mag kein/keine(n) (+ noun)/Ich (+ verb) nicht gern

ikh mark kain/kainer(n)/ikh...nikht gayrn

I'm bored to death _____ Ich langweile mich furchtbar

ikh langvailer mikh foorkhtbar

I've had enough _____ Mir reicht's

meer raikhts

I was expecting _____ Ich hatte etwas ganz anderes erwartet
something completely *ikh hatter etvass gants andererz airvartet*
different

3 Conversation

3.1 I beg your pardon?

I don't speak any/ ____ I speak a little...	Ich spreche kein/ein bisschen... *ikh shprekher kain/ain bisskhen...*
I'm English ____	Ich bin Engländer/in *ikh bin englender (male)/englenderi (female)*
I'm Scottish ____	Ich bin Schotte/Schottin *ikh bin shotter/shottin*
I'm Irish ____	Ich bin Irländer/Irländerin *ikh bin earlender/earlenderin*
I'm Welsh ____	Ich bin Waliser/Waliserin *ikh bin valeezer/valeezerin*
Do you speak ____ English/French/ German?	Sprechen Sie Englisch/Französisch/Deutsch? *shprekhen zee english/frantsoezish/doytsh?*
Is there anyone who ____ speaks...?	Ist hier jemand, der ... spricht? *ist heer yaymant, dayr ... shprikht?*
I beg your pardon? ____	Wie bitte? *vee bitter?*
I (don't) understand ____	Ich verstehe (es) (nicht) *ikh fair shtayher (es) (nikht)*
Do you understand ____ me?	Verstehen Sie mich? *fair shtayhen zee mikh?*
Could you repeat that, _ please?	Würden Sie das bitte wiederholen? *vuerden zee dass bitter vee-der-hoalen?*
Could you speak more _ slowly, please?	Könnten Sie etwas langsamer sprechen? *koennten zee etvass langzarmer shprekhen?*
What does that (word) ____ mean?	Was bedeutet das/dieses Wort? *vass bedoytet dass/deezez vort?*
Is that similar to/the ____ same as...?	Ist das (ungefähr) dasselbe wie..? *ist dass (oongefair) dass zelber vee..?*
Could you write that ____ down for me, please?	Könnten Sie mir das bitte aufschreiben? *koennten zee meer dass bitter owfshraiben?*

| Could you spell that ___ for me, please? | Könnten Sie mir das bitte buchstabieren? |
| | *koennten zee meer dass bitter bookhshtabeeren?* |

(See 1.8 Telephone alphabet)

Could you point that ___ out in this phrase book, please?	Könnten Sie mir das in diesem Sprachführer zeigen?
	koennten zee meer dass in deezem shprakhfuerer tsaigen?
One moment, please, ___ I have to look it up	Augenblick bitte, ich muß es erst suchen
	owgenblick bitte, ikh mooss ez erst zookhen
I can't find the_____ word/the sentence	Ich kann das Wort/den Satz nicht finden
	ikh kann dass vort/dayn zats nikht finden
How do you say _____ that in...?	Wie sagt man das auf...
	vee zarkt mann dass owf...
How do you_____ pronounce that?	Wie spricht man das aus?
	vee shprikht mann dass ows?

3.2 Introductions

May I introduce_____ myself?	Darf ich mich Ihnen vorstellen?
	darf ikh mikh eenen forshtellen?
My name's... _____	Ich heisse...
	ikh haisser...
I'm... _____	Ich bin...
	ikh bin...
What's your name? ____	Wie heissen Sie?
	vee haissen zee?
May I introduce...?_____	Darf ich Ihnen vorstellen...?
	darf ikh eenen forshtellen...?

This is my wife/ _____ daughter/mother/ girlfriend	Dies ist meine Frau/Tochter/Mutter/Freundin *deez ist mainer frow/tokhter/mootter/froyndin*
– my husband/son/ ____ father/boyfriend	Dies ist mein Mann/Sohn/Vater/Freund. *dees ist main mann/zoan/farter/froynt.*
How do you do_____	Guten Tag/Abend, nett Sie kennenzulernen *gooten tark/arbent, nett zee kennen tsoo layrnen*
Pleased to meet you ___	Angenehm *angenaym*
Where are you from?___	Woher kommen Sie? *voahair kommen zee?*
I'm from _____ England/Scotland/ Ireland/Wales	Ich komme aus England/Schottland/Irland/Wales *ikh kommer ows englant/shottlant/earlant/vaylz*
What city do you _____ live in?	In welcher Stadt wohnen Sie? *in velkher shtatt voanen zee?*
In..., It ís near... _____	In.... Das ist in der Nähe von... *in.... dass ist in dayr nayher fon...*
Have you been here ___ long?	Sind Sie schon lange hier? *zint zee shoan langer heer?*
A few days_____	Ein paar Tage *ain pahr targer*
How long are you_____ staying here?	Wie lange bleiben Sie hier? *vee langer blaiben zee heer?*
We're (probably) _____ leaving tomorrow/ in two weeks	Wir reisen (wahrscheinlich) morgen/in zwei Wochen ab *veer raizen (varshainlikh) morgun/in tsvai vokhen ap*
Where are you _____ staying?	Wo wohnen Sie? *vo voanen zee?*
In a hotel/an apartment_	In einem Hotel/Appartement *in ainem hotel/apartament*

On a camp site	Auf einem Campingplatz
	owf ainem camping plats
With friends/relatives	Bei Freunden/Verwandten
	bai froynden/fairvanten
Are you here on your own/with your family?	Sind Sie hier allein/mit Ihrer Familie?
	zint zee heer allain/mit eerer fameelyeh?
I'm on my own	Ich bin allein
	ikh bin allain
I'm with my partner/wife/husband	Ich bin hier mit meinem Partner/meiner Partnerin/meiner Frau/meinem Mann
	ikh bin heer mit mainem partner/mainer partnerin/mainer frow/mainem man
– with my family	Ich bin hier mit meiner Familie
	ikh bin hier mit mainer fameelyeh
– with relatives	Ich bin hier mit Verwandten
	ikh bin hier mit fairvanten
– with a friend/friends	Ich bin hier mit einem Freund/einer Freundin/Freunden
	ikh bin hier mit ainem froynt/ainer froyndin/froynden
Are you married?	Sind Sie verheiratet?
	zint zee fairhairartet?
Do you have a steady boyfriend/girlfriend?	Hast du eine feste Freundin/einen festen Freund?
	hast doo ainer fester froyndin/aynen festen froynt?
That's none of your business	Das geht Sie nichts an
	dass gayt zee nikhts an
I'm married	Ich bin verheiratet
	ikh bin fairhai rartet
– single	Ich bin Junggeselle/Junggesellin
	ikh bin yoong ge zeller/yoong ge zellin
– separated	Ich lebe getrennt
	ikh layber getrennt
– divorced	Ich bin geschieden
	ikh bin gesheeden

– a widow/widower _____	Ich bin Witwe/Witwer
	ikh bin vitveh/vitver
I live alone/with_____	Ich lebe allein/mit jemandem zusammen
someone	*ikh layber allain/mit yaymandem*
	tsoozammen
Do you have any _____	Haben Sie Kinder/Enkel?
children/grandchildren?	*harben zee kinder/enkell?*
How old are you?_____	Wie alt sind Sie?
	vee alt zint zee?
How old is he/she? ____	Wie alt ist er/sie?
	vee alt ist ayr/zee?
I'm... _____	Ich bin ... Jahre alt
	ikh bin ... yahrer alt
She's/he's..._____	Sie/er ist ... Jahre alt
	zee/ayr ist ... yahrer alt
What do you do for a __	Was für eine Arbeit machen Sie?
living?	*vass fuer ainer arbait makhen zee?*
I work in an office_____	Ich arbeite in einem Büro
	ikh arbaiter in ainem buero
I'm a student/ _____	Ich studiere/gehe zur Schule
I'm at school	*ikh shtoodearer/gayher tsoor shooler*
I'm unemployed _____	Ich bin arbeitslos
	ikh bin arbaitsloaz
I'm retired _____	Ich bin pensioniert/Rentner/Rentnerin
	ikh bin pen zeeoa neert/rentner/rentnerin
I have taken early_____	Ich bin im Vorruhestand
retirement	*ikh bin im for-rooher-shtant*
I'm on a disability_____	Ich habe eine Erwerbsunfähigkeitsrente
pension	*ikh harber ainer erverps oon fayikh kaits*
	renter
I'm a housewife _____	Ich bin Hausfrau
	ikh bin howzfrow
Do you like your job? __	Macht Ihnen die Arbeit Spass?
	makht eenen dee arbait shpass?

Most of the time _____	Mal ja, mal nein
	marl yar, marl nain
I usually do, but I _____ prefer holidays	Meistens schon, aber Urlaub ist schöner
	maistens shoan, arber oorlowp ist shoener

3.3 Starting/ending a conversation

Could I ask you _____ something?	Dürfte ich Sie etwas fragen?
	duerfter ikh zee etvass frargen?
Excuse me _____	Entschuldigen Sie bitte
	ent shool digen zee bitter
Excuse me, could you _____ help me?	Entschuldigung, könnten Sie mir helfen?
	ent shool digoong, koennten zee meer helfen?
Yes, what's the _____ problem?	Ja, was ist denn los?
	yar, vass ist den loas?
What can I do for you? _____	Was kann ich für Sie tun?
	vass kan ikh fuer zee toon?
Sorry, I don't have time _____ now	Bedaure, ich habe jetzt keine Zeit
	bedowrer, ikh harber yetst kainer tsayt
Do you have a light? _____	Haben Sie Feuer?
	harben zee foyerr?
May I join you? _____	Darf ich mich zu Ihnen setzen?
	darf ikh mikh tsoo eenen zetsen?
Could you take a _____ picture of me/us?	Würden Sie ein Foto von mir/uns machen?
	vuerden zee ain foto fon meer/oons makhen?
Leave me alone _____	Lassen Sie mich in Ruhe
	lassen zee mikh in rooher
Get lost _____	Machen Sie, daß Sie wegkommen
	makhen zee dass zee vek kommen
Go away or I'll scream _____	Wenn Sie nicht weggehen, schrei' ich
	ven zee nikht vek gayhen, shrai ikh

3.4 Congratulations and condolences

Happy birthday/many __
happy returns

Meinen Glückwunsch zum Geburtstag
mainen gluekvoonsh tsoom geboortstark

Please accept my _____
condolences

Mein Beileid
main bailait

I'm very sorry for you __

Es tut mir ja so leid für Sie
ez toot meer yar zo lait fuer zee

3.5 A chat about the weather

See also 1.5 The weather

It's so hot/cold today! __

Heute ist es aber warm/kalt!
hoyter ist ez arber varm/kalt!

Nice weather, isn't it? __

Angenehmes Wetter, nicht?
angenaymers vetter, nikht?

What a wind/storm! ____

So ein Wind/Sturm!
zo ain vint/shtoorm

All that rain/snow! _____

Wie das regnet/schneit!
vee dass raygnet/shnait!

All that fog! _____

Das ist vielleicht ein Nebel!
dass ist feelaikht ain naybel!

Has the weather been __
like this for long here?

Ist das Wetter hier schon lange so?
ist dass vetter heer shoan langer zo?

Is it always this_____
hot/cold here?

Ist es hier immer so warm/kalt?
ist es heer immer zo varm/kalt?

Is it always this_____
dry/wet here?

Ist es hier immer so trocken/nass?
ist es heer immer zo trokken/nass?

3.6 Hobbies

Do you have any _____
hobbies?

Haben Sie Hobbys?
harben zee hobbies?

I like knitting/_____ reading/photography/ painting	Ich stricke/lese/fotografiere/zeichne gern *ikh shtrikker/layzer/fotograffearer/tsaikhner gayrn*
I like music _____	Ich liebe Musik *ikh leeber moozeek*
I like playing the _____ guitar/piano	Ich spiele gern Gitarre/Klavier *ikh shpeeler gayrn gitarrer/klaveer*
I like going to the _____ movies	Ich gehe gern ins Kino *ikh gayher gayrn ins keeno*
I like travelling/ _____ fishing/walking/sport	Ich reise/angle/wandre gern *ikh raizer/angler/vanderer gayrn*

3.7 Being the host(ess)

See also 4 Eating out

Can I offer you a _____ drink?	Darf ich Ihnen etwas zu trinken anbieten? *darf ikh eenen etvass tsoo trinken anbeeten?*
What would you like ___ to drink?	Was möchtest du trinken? *vass moekhtest doo trinken?*
Would you like a_____ cigarette/cigar?	Möchten Sie eine Zigarette/Zigarre? *moekhten zee ainer tsigarretter/tsigarrer?*
Something non- _____ alcoholic,please	Gern etwas ohne Alkohol *gayrn etvass oaner alkohol*
I don't smoke _____	Ich rauche nicht *ikh rowkher nikht*

3.8 Invitations

| Are you doing anything_ tonight? | Hast du heute abend was vor? *hast doo hoyter arbent vass for?* |
| Do you have any plans _ for today/this afternoon/tonight? | Haben Sie schon Pläne für heute/heute nachmittag/heute abend? *harben zee shoan playner fuer hoyter/hoyter nakhmittark/hoyter arbent?* |

Would you like to go ___ out with me?	Haben Sie Lust, mit mir auszugehen? *harben zee loost, mit meer ows tsoo gayhen?*
Would you like to go ___ dancing with me?	Haben Sie Lust, mit mir tanzen zu gehen? *harben zee loost, mitt meer tantsen tsoo gayhen?*
Would you like to have _ lunch/dinner with me?	Haben Sie Lust, mit mir zu essen? *harben zee loost, mit meer tsoo essen?*
Would you like to _____ come to the beach with me?	Haben Sie Lust, an den Strand zu gehen? *harben zee loost, an den shtrant tsoo gayhen?*
Would you like to _____ come into town with us?	Haben Sie Lust, mit uns in die Stadt zu gehen/fahren? *harben zee loost, mit oons in dee shtatt tsoo gayhen/fahren?*
Would you like to _____ come and see some friends with us?	Haben Sie Lust, mit uns zu Freunden zu gehen? *harben zee loost, mit oons tsoo froynden tsoo gayhen?*
Shall we dance?_____	Wollen wir tanzen? *vollen veer tantsen?*
– sit at the bar? _____	Kommst du mit an die Bar? *kommst doo mit an dee bar?*
– get something to ____ drink?	Wollen wir etwas trinken? *vollen veer etvass trinken?*
– go for a walk/drive? __	Wollen wir ein bisschen spazierengehen/Auto fahren? *vollen veer ain bisskhen shpatseeren gayhen/owto fahren?*
Yes, all right_____	Ja, gut *yar, goot*
Good idea _____	Gute Idee *gooter eeday*
No (thank you) _____	Nein (danke) *nain (dunker)*
Maybe later _____	Vielleicht später *feelaikht shpayter*
I don't feel like it_____	Dazu habe ich keine Lust *datsoo harber ikh kainer loost*

I don't have time _____	Ich habe keine Zeit
	ikh harber kainer tsait
I already have a date ___	Ich habe schon eine Verabredung
	ikh harber shoan ainer fair ap ray doong
I'm not very good at ___ dancing/volleyball/ swimming	Ich kann nicht tanzen/Volleyball spielen/schwimmen
	ikh kann nikht tantsen/volleyball shpeelen/shvimmen

3.9 Paying a compliment

You look wonderful! _____	Sie sehen (ja) fabelhaft aus!
	zee zayhen (yar) farbelhaft ows!
I like your car! _____	Schönes/tolles Auto!
	shoenez/tollez owto!
I like your ski outfit! ____	Hübscher Skianzug!
	huepsher shee antsook!
You're a nice boy/girl ___	Du bist lieb
	doo bist leep
What a sweet child! ____	Was für ein liebes Kind!
	vass fuer ain leebes kint!
You're a wonderful _____ dancer!	Sie tanzen sehr gut!
	zee tantsen zayr goot!
You're a wonderful _____ cook!	Sie kochen sehr gut!
	zee kokhen zayr goot!
You're a terrific soccer _ player!	Sie spielen sehr gut Fussball!
	zee shpeelen zayr goot foossball!

3.10 Chatting someone up

I like being with you _____	Ich bin gern mit dir zusammen
	ikh bin gayrn mit deer tsoozammen
I've missed you so _____ much	Ich habe dich so vermisst
	ikh haber dikh zo fairmisst

English	German / Pronunciation
dreamt about you ____	Ich habe von dir geträumt *ikh haber fon deer getroymt*
think about you _____ all day	Ich muss den ganzen Tag an dich denken *ikh muss den gantsen tark an dikh denken*
You have such a sweet _ smile	Du lächelst so süss *doo laekhelst zo suess*
You have such _____ beautiful eyes	Du hast so schöne Augen *doo hast zo shoener owgen*
I'm in love with you ____	Ich habe mich in dich verliebt *ikh haber mikh in dikh fairleept*
I'm in love with you too_	Ich mich auch in dich *ikh mikh owkh in dikh*
I love you_____	Ich liebe dich *ikh leeber dikh*
I love you too _____	Ich dich auch *ikh dikh owkh*
I don't feel as strongly__ about you	Ich empfinde nicht dasselbe für dich *ikh empfinder nikht dass selber fuer dikh*
I already have a _____ boyfriend/girlfriend	Ich habe schon einen Freund/ein Freundin *ikh harber shoan ainen froynt/ainer froyndin*
I'm not ready for that___	Ich bin noch nicht so weit *ikh bin nokh nikht zo vait*
This is going too fast___ for me	Es geht mir viel zu schnell *ez gayt meer feel tsoo shnell*
Take your hands_____ off me	Rühr mich nicht an *ruehr mikh nikht an*
Okay, no problem_____	O.k., kein Problem *oakay, kain problaym*
Will you stay with me __ tonight?	Bleibst du heute nacht bei mir? *blaipst doo hoyter nakht bai meer?*
I'd like to go to bed ____ with you	Ich möchte mit dir schlafen *ikh moekhter mit deer shlarfen*
Only if we use a _____ condom	Nur mit Präservativ/Kondom *noor mitt prezervatif/kondoam*

We have to be careful __ about AIDS	Wir müssen vorsichtig sein wegen Aids *veer muessen forsikhtik zain vaygen aids*
That's what they_____ all say	Das sagen alle *dass zargen aller*
We shouldn't take any__ risks	Wir wollen lieber kein Risiko eingehen *veer vollen leeber kain reeziko aingayhen*
Do you have a _____ condom?	Hast du ein Präservativ/Kondom? *hast doo ain prezervatif/kondoam?*
No? In that case we ___ won't do it	Nein? Dann machen wir's nicht *nain? dann makhen veer's nikht*

3.11 Arrangements

When will I see _____ you again?	Wann sehe ich Sie/dich wieder? *vann zayher ikh zee/dikh veeder?*
Are you free over the___ weekend?	Haben Sie am Wochenende Zeit? *harben zee am vokhenender tsait?*
What shall we _____ arrange?	Wie verbleiben wir? *vee fairblaiben veer?*
Where shall we meet?__	Wo wollen wir uns treffen? *voa vollen veer oons treffen?*
Will you pick _____ me/us up?	Holen Sie mich/uns ab? *hoalen zee mikh/oons ap?*
Shall I pick you up?____	Soll ich Sie abholen? *zoll ikh zee apholen?*
I have to be home by... _	Ich muss um...Uhr zu Hause sein *ikh muss oom...ooer tsoo howzer zain*
I don't want to see_____ you anymore	Ich will Sie nicht mehr sehen *ikh vill zee nikht mayr zayhen*

English	German	Pronunciation
Can I take you home?	Darf ich Sie nach Hause bringen?	darf ikh zee nakh howzer bringen?
Can I write/call you?	Darf ich Ihnen schreiben/Sie anrufen?	darf ikh eenen shraiben/zee anroofen?
Will you write/call me?	Schreiben Sie mir/rufen Sie mich an?	shraiben zee meer/roofen zee mikh an?
Can I have your address/phone number?	Geben Sie mir Ihre Adresse/Telefonnummer?	gayben zee meer eerer adresser/telefoan noomer?
Thanks for everything	Vielen Dank für alles	feelen dunk fuer alless
It was very nice	Es war sehr schön	es var zayr shoen
Say hello to...	Grüssen Sie...	gruessen zee...
All the best	Alles Gute	alles gooter
Good luck	Viel Erfolg weiter	feel erfolk vaiter
When will you be back?	Wann kommst du wieder?	vann kommst doo veeder?
I'll be waiting for you	Ich warte auf dich	ikh varter owf dikh
I'd like to see you again	Ich möchte dich gern wiedersehen	ikh moekhter dikh gayrn veeder zayhen
I hope we meet again soon	Ich hoffe, wir sehen uns wieder	ikh hoffer, veer zayhen oons veeder
This is our address. If you're ever in the UK...	Dies ist unsere Adresse. Wenn Sie je in Grossbritannien sind...	deez ist oonzerer adresser. venn zee yay in englant zint...
You'd be more than welcome	Sie sind uns herzlich willkommen	zee zint oons hertslikh villkommen

● **In Germany** people usually have three main meals:

1 *Frühstück* (breakfast) between approx. 6.30 and 10am. Breakfast is varied and can consist of coffee or herbal infusions, cereal (particularly muesli), bread rolls or slices of *Vollkornbrot* (whole-wheat bread) with a choice of butter, jam, ham or cheese. On Sundays this array is often complemented by boiled eggs.

2 *Mittagessen* (lunch) approx. between midday and 2pm. Traditionally lunch consists of a hot dish and is the most important meal of the day. Offices and shops often close while lunch is taken at home, in a restaurant or canteen. It usually consists of two or three courses:
- starter
- main course
- dessert

3 *Abendessen* (dinner)/*Vesper* (cold evening meal in southern Germany) between 6 and 9.30pm. This either consists of a light hot meal or a cold meal such as slices of bread with cold meat, cheese and salad.

At about 3.30pm particularly on a Sunday coffee and all kinds of cakes and pastries are taken.

4.1 On arrival

I'd like to book a table for seven o'clock, please	Kann ich einen Tisch für sieben Uhr reservieren lassen? *kann ikh ainen tish fuer zeeben ooer rezerveeren lassen?*
I'd like a table for two, please	Bitte einen Tisch für zwei Personen *bitter ainen tish fuer tsvai perzoanen*
We've/we haven't booked	Wir haben (nicht) reserviert *veer harben (nikht) rezerveert*
Is the restaurant open yet?	Hat die Küche schon geöffnet? *hat dee kuekher shoan geoeffnet?*
What time does the restaurant open/close?	Wann öffnet/schliesst die Küche? *vann oeffnet/shleest dee kuekher?*

Haben Sie reserviert?	*Do you have a reservation?*
Unter welchem Namen?	*What name, please?*
Hierher bitte	*This way, please*
Dieser Tisch ist reserviert	*This table is reserved*
In einer Viertelstunde wird ein Tisch frei	*We'll have a table free in fifteen minutes*
Möchten Sie solange (an der Bar) warten?	*Would you like to wait (at the bar)?*

Can we wait for a_____ table?	Können wir auf einen Tisch warten? *koennen veer owf ainen tish varten?*
Do we have to wait ____ long?	Müssen wir lange warten? *muessen veer langer varten?*
Is this seat taken? _____	Ist dieser Platz frei? *ist deezer plats frai?*
Could we sit _____ here/there?	Können wir uns hierher/dahin setzen? *koennen veer oons heerhair/darhin zetsen?*
Can we sit by the_____ window?	Können wir uns ans Fenster setzen? *koennen veer oons ans fenster zetsen?*
Can we eat outside? ___	Können wir auch draussen essen? *koennen veer owkh drowsen essen?*
Do you have another ___ chair for us?	Könnten Sie uns noch einen Stuhl bringen? *koennten zee oons nokh ainen shtool bringen?*
Do you have a highchair? _____	Könnten Sie uns einen Kinderstuhl bringen? *koennten zee oons ainen kindershtool bringen?*
Is there a socket for____ this bottle-warmer?	Gibt es für diesen Flaschenwärmer eine Steckdose? *gipt es fuer deezen flashen vayrmerr ainer shtekdozer?*

Could you warm up ___ this bottle/jar for me?	Könnten Sie mir dieses Fläschchen/Gläschen aufwärmen?
	koennten zee meer deezez fleshkhen/glayzkhen owfvermen?
Not too hot, please ___	Nicht zu heiss bitte
	nikht tsoo haiss bitter
Is there somewhere I ___ can change the baby's nappy?	Gibt es hier einen Raum, wo ich das Baby wickeln kann?
	gipt ez heer ainen rowm vo ikh dass bayby vikkeln kann?
Where are the toilets? ___	Wo ist die Toilette?
	vo ist dee twaletter?

4.2 Ordering

Waiter! _____	Herr Ober!
	herr oaber!
Madam! _____	Bedienung!
	bedeenoong!
Sir! _____	Bitte!
	bitter!
We'd like something to ___ eat/a drink	Wir möchten gern etwas essen/trinken
	veer moekhten gayrn etvass essen/trinken
Could I have a quick ___ meal?	Könnte ich schnell etwas essen?
	koennter ikh shnell etvass essen?
We don't have much time_____	Wir haben wenig Zeit
	veer harben vaynikh tsait
We'd like to have a ___ drink first	Wir möchten erst noch etwas trinken
	veer moekhten ayrst nokh etvass trinken
Could we see the_____ menu/wine list, please?	Wir hätten gern die Speisekarte/Weinkarte/(Getränkekarte)
	veer hetten gayrn dee spaizer karter/vain karter(gertrenker karte)

Do you have a menu ___ in English?	Haben Sie eine Speisekarte in Englisch?
	harben zee ainer shpayzer karter in english?
Do you have a dish ___ of the day?	Haben Sie ein Tagesmenü/Touristenmenü?
	harben zee ain targes menyoo/toorissten menyoo?
We haven't made a ___ choice yet	Wir haben noch nicht gewählt
	veer harben nokh nikht gevaylt
What do you ___ recommend?	Was können Sie uns empfehlen?
	vass koennen zee oons empfaylen?
What are the ___ specialities of the region/the house?	Welches sind die Spezialitäten dieser Gegend/des Hauses?
	velkhes zint dee shpetseeali tayten deezer gegent/dez howzez?
I like strawberries/ ___ olives	Ich liebe Erdbeeren/Oliven
	ikh leeber ertbeeren/olleeven
I don't like meat/fish/... ___	Ich mag kein Fleisch/keinen Fisch
	ikh mark kain flaish/kainen fish
What's this? ___	Was ist das?
	vass ist dass?
Does it have...in it? ___	Ist das mit...?
	ist dass mit...?
What does it taste ___ like?	Womit kann man das vergleichen?
	vo-mitt kann mann dass fairglaikhen?

Möchten Sie essen/speisen?	*Would you like to eat?*
Haben Sie schon gewählt?	*Have you decided?*
Möchten Sie eine Nachspeise?	*Would you like a dessert?*
Was darf es sein?	*What would you like?*
Guten Appetit!	*Enjoy your meal*
Darf/Dürfte ich jetzt abrechnen?	*May I ask you to settle the bill, please?*

Is this a hot or a _____ cold dish?	Ist dieses Gericht warm oder kalt? *ist deezes gerikht varm oader kalt?*
Is this sweet? _____	Ist es eine Süßspeise? *ist ez ainer suess shpaizer?*
Is this spicy? _____	Ist es pikant/scharf? *ist es peekant/sharf?*
Do you have anything __ else, please?	Haben Sie vielleicht etwas anderes? *harben zee feelaihkt etvass anderez?*
I'm on a salt-free diet __	Ich darf kein Salz essen *ikh darf kain zalts essen*
I can't eat pork _____	Ich darf kein Schweinefleisch essen *ikh darf kain shvainer flaish essen*
– sugar _____	Ich darf keinen Zucker essen *ikh darf kainen tsooker essen*
– fatty foods _____	Ich darf kein Fett essen *ikh darf kain fet essen*
– (hot) spices_____	Ich darf keine scharfen Gewürze essen *ikh darf kainer sharfen gewuertser essen*
I'll/we'll have what _____ those people are having	Ich möchte/wir möchten gern dasselbe wie die Leute da *ikh moekhter/veer moekhten gayrn dass selber vee dee loyter dar*
I'd like... _____	Ich möchte... *ikh moekhter...*
We're not having a_____ starter	Wir nehmen keine Vorspeise *veer naymen kainer for shpaizer*
The child will share _____ what we're having	Das Kind isst etwas von unserem Menü mit *dass kint ist etvass fon oonzerem menyoo mit*
Could I have some_____ more bread, please?	Noch etwas Brot bitte *nokh etvass broat bitter*
– a bottle of water/wine	Noch eine Flasche (Mineral)wasser/Wein bitte *nokh ainer flasher (minerarl)vasser/vain bitter*

– another helping of... _	Noch eine Portion....bitte *nokh ainer portseeoan...bitter*
– some salt and _____ pepper	Würden Sie bitte Salz und Pfeffer bringen? *vuerden zee bitter zalts unt pfeffer bringen?*
– a napkin _____	Würden Sie bitte eine Serviette bringen? *vuerden zee bitter ainer zerviyetter bringen?*
– a spoon_____	Würden Sie bitte einen Löffel bringen? *vuerden zee bitter ainen loeffel bringen?*
– an ashtray_____	Würden Sie bitte einen Aschenbecher bringen? *vuerden zee bitter ainen ashen bekher bringen?*
– some matches_____	Würden Sie bitte Streichhölzer bringen? *vuerden zee bitter shtraikh hoeltser bringen?*
– a glass of water_____	Würden Sie bitte ein Glas Wasser bringen? *vuerden zee bitter ain glars vasser bringen?*
– a straw (for the child) _	Würden Sie bitte (für das Kind) einen Trinkhalm bringen? *vuerden zee bitter (fuer dass kint) ainen trinkhalm bringen?*
Enjoy your meal!_____	Guten Appetit! *gooten appeteet!*
You too! _____	Danke, gleichfalls *dunker, glaikhfals*
Cheers!_____	Prost/zum Wohl! *prrosst/tsoom voal!*
The next round's _____ on me	Die nächste Runde gebe ich (aus) *dee nexter roonder gayber ikh (ows)*
Could we have a _____ doggy bag, please?	Dürfen wir die Reste mitnehmen? *duerfen veer dee rester mitnaymen?*

4.3 The bill

See also 8.2 Settling the bill

How much is this _____ dish?	Wieviel kostet dieses Gericht? *veefeel kostet deezes gerikht?*
Could I have the bill, ___ please?	Die Rechnung bitte *dee rekhnoong bitter*
All together _____	Alles zusammen *alles tsoozammen*
Everyone pays _____ separately	Getrennt zahlen *getrennt tsarlen*
Could we have the_____ menu again, please?	Dürften wir die Karte noch mal sehen? *duerften veer dee karter nokh marl zayhen?*
The...is not on the bill __	Der/die/das...steht nicht auf der Rechnung *der/dee/dass...shtayt nihkt owf dayr rekhnoong*

4.4 Complaints

It's taking a very _____ long time	Das dauert aber lange *dass dowert arber langer*
We've been here an____ hour already	Wir sitzen hier schon seit einer Stunde *veer zitsen heer shoan zait ainer shtoonder*
This must be a mistake_	Das muss ein Irrtum sein *dass muss ain eartoom zain*
This is not what I _____ ordered	Das habe ich nicht bestellt *dass harber ikh nikht beshtellt*
I ordered... _____	Ich habe um...gebeten *ikh harber oom...gebayten*
There's a dish missing__	Es fehlt ein Gericht *ez faylt ain gerikht*
This is broken/ _____ not clean	Das ist kaputt/nicht sauber *dass ist kapoott/nikht zowber*

The food's cold _____	Das Essen ist kalt
	dass essen ist kalt
– not fresh _____	Das Essen ist nicht frisch
	dass essen ist nikht frish
– too salty/sweet/spicy _	Das Essen ist versalzen/zu süss/scharf
	dass essen ist fairzaltsen/tsoo zuess/sharf
The meat's not done ___	Das Fleisch ist nicht gar
	dass flaish ist nikht garr
– overdone _____	Das Fleisch ist zu sehr durchgebraten
	dass flaish ist tsoo zayr doorkh gebrarten
– tough_____	Das Fleisch ist zäh
	dass flaish ist tsay
– off_____	Das Fleisch ist verdorben
	dass flaish ist fairdorben
Could I have _____ something else instead of this?	Können Sie mir hierfür etwas anderes bringen?
	koennen zee meer heerfuerr etvass anderez bringen?
The bill/this amount is_ not right	Die Rechnung/dieser Betrag stimmt nicht
	dee rekhnoong/deezer betrark shtimmt nikht
We didn't have this ____	Das haben wir nicht gehabt
	dass harben veer nihkt gehapt
There's no paper in the toilet_____	Auf der Toilette ist kein Toilettenpapier
	owf der twaletter ist kain twaletten papeer
Do you have a _____ complaints book?	haben Sie ein Beschwerdebuch
	harben zee ain beshverder bookh?
Will you call the _____ manager, please?	Würden Sie bitte den Chef rufen?
	vuerden zee bitter den shef roofen?

4.5 Paying a compliment

That was a wonderful __ meal — Wir haben herrlich gegessen
veer harben hairlikh gegessen

The food was excellent_ — Es hat uns ausgezeichnet geschmeckt
ez hat oons owsge tsaikhnet geshmekt

The...in particular was__ delicious — Vor allem der/die/das...war hervorragend
for allem dayr/dee/dass...var hair for rargent

4.6 The menu

Bedienung einschliesslich
service included
Beilagen
side-dishes
Erfrischungsgetränke
refreshment drinks
Fisch
fish
Frühstück
breakfast
Gebäck
biscuits, pastries, buns, tarts, tartlets
Gedeck
set meal/place
Gerichte
dishes

Getränke (karte)
beverages/list of beverages (café) or wine list (restaurant)
Happen snack
Hauptgerichte
main courses
Köstlichkeiten
delicacies
Kuchen
cake(s)
Meeresfrüchte
seafood
Nachspeisen
desserts
Spezialitäten
specialities

Suppen
soups
Tagesmenü
menu of the day
Tagesteller
dish of the day
Torten
gateau/flan (with fruit)
Vorspeisen
starters
Weine
wines
Weinkarte
wine list
Zwischengerichte
entrée/snack

4.7 Alphabetical list of drinks and dishes

Aal
eel

Apfel
apple

Äpfel im Schlafrock
baked apples in puff
pastry

Apfelsine
orange

Aspik
aspic

Aufschnitt
sliced cold meat or
(rarer) cheese

Austern
oysters

Bauern-
farmer's/rustic

-brot
coarse rye bread

-frühstück
bacon and potato
omelette

Beeren
berries

Birne
pears

Bismarckhering
Bismarck herring
(filleted pickled
herring)

Blaubeere
blueberry

Blaukraut
red cabbage

Bohnen (grüne,
grosse)
green beans

Braten
roast

Bratkartoffeln
fried potatoes

Brause
pop/lemonade

Bries(chen), Briesel
dish containing
sweetbreads of
animals (mostly
calves)

Brombeere
blackberry

Brot
bread

Brötchen
bread rolls

Brühe
clear soup/stock

Brust
breast

Bündner Fleisch
smoked ham from
the region of
Graubünden in
Switzerland

Butt
flounder/butt

Butter
butter

Chicoree
chicory

Curry
curry

Dampfnudeln
sweet yeast
dumpling cooked in
milk and sugar

Dattel
date

Dörr-
dried

Dorsch
cod

Eierkuchen (dünn)
(thin) pancakes

Eierstich
egg based ingredient
of some soups

Eintopf
stew

Eisbecher
sundae(s)

Eisbombe
ice cream cake

Endivie
endive

Ente
duck

Erbsen
peas

German	English
Erdbeere	strawberry
Essig	vinegar
Fadennudeln	vermicelli
Feige	fig
Filetsteak	fillet steak
Fisch	fish
Fisolen	green beans
Fleisch	meat
Flusskrebs	crayfish
Frikassee (Hühner-)	(chicken) fricassee
Frittatensuppe	soup containing strips of pancake
Frühlingsrolle	spring rolls
Gänseleber	goose liver
Garnele	shrimp
gebraten	fried
gedünstet	braised
Geflügel	poultry
gefüllt	filled/stuffed
gekocht	boiled
Gelee	jelly
Gemüse	vegetables
geräuchert	smoked
Geschnetzeltes	meat cut into strips stewed to produce a thick sauce
Geselchtes	salted and smoked meat
gespickt	larded/fried meat with strips of bacon
getrocknet	dried
gewürzt	seasoned
Glühwein	mulled wine
Grog	grog
Gulasch	goulash
Gurke (saure-)	(pickled) gherkins
Hähnchen/Hühnchen	chicken
Hase	hare
Haselnuss	hazelnut
Hasenpfeffer	jugged hare
Hering	herring
Heurige(r)	new wine
Himbeere	raspberry
Hirn	brains
Hirsch	venison
Hummer	lobster
Ingwer	ginger
Jause	snack
Johannisbeere	blackcurrant/redcurrant
Kalb	calf
Kaldaunen/Kutteln	tripe
Kaltschale	cold sweet soup
Kaninchen	rabbit
Karfiol	cauliflower
Karotten	carrots
Karpfen	carp

Kartoffel	potato
Kartoffelpuffer	potato fritter
Käse	cheese
Kekse	biscuits
Keule	leg
Kirsche	cherry
Klösse (Kartoffel-, Semmel-)	dumplings (potato, bread)
Knoblauch	garlic
Knödel	dumplings
Knusprig	crisp/crunchy
Kochschinken	boiled ham
Kompott	stewed fruit/compote
Konfitüre	jam
Korn	corn/corn schnapps
Krabbe	crab
Krapfen	doughnut
Kräuter-	herbal
Labskaus	stew made of meat, fish and mashed potato
Lachs	salmon
Languste	crayfish
Lauch	leek
Lebkuchen	gingerbread
Likör	liqueur
Mandel	almond
Marille	apricot
mariniert	marinated
Marone	chestnut
Maultaschen	filled pasta squares
Meerrettich	horseradish
Melone	melon
Mett	minced pork/beef
Milch	milk
Muscheln	mussels
Nockerl	little dumplings
Nougat	nougat
Obst (je nach Jahreszeit/ Saison)	fruit (of the season)
Obstkuchen	fruitcake
Obstler	fruit schnapps
Ochsenschwanz	oxtail
Öl	oil
Orange	orange
Palatschinken	stuffed pancake
Pampelmuse	grapefruit
Pastete	paté
Petersilie	parsley
Pfannkuchen	pancake
Pfeffer	pepper
Pfifferling	chanterelle
Pfirsich	peach
Pflaume	plum
Pilze	mushrooms

Platte	plate
Plätzchen	biscuit/cookie
Pommes frites	French fries
Porree	leek
Preßsack	a type of cold meat
Pute	turkey
Quark	(soft) curd cheese
Radieschen	radish
Rahm	cream
Räucherschinken	smoked ham
Rebhuhn	partridge
Reh	deer
Reibekuchen	potato waffle
Reis	rice
Remoulade	remoulade
resch (rösch)	crisp/crusty
Rinder-	beef
Rinderfilet	beef fillet
Rindfleisch	beef
Rippe	rib
roh	raw
Rosenkohl	Brussels sprouts
Rosine	raisin
Rostbraten	roast
Röstkartoffeln	fried potatoes
rote Beete	beetroot
Rührei	scrambled eggs
Rumpsteak	rump steak
Sachertorte	a rich chocolate cake
Saft	juice
Sahne	cream
Salat (gemischt)	salad (mixed)
Salzkartoffeln	boiled potatoes
Sauerkraut	sauerkraut/pickled cabbage
Schaum-	frothy
Schildkrötensuppe	turtle soup
Schinken	ham
Schlagobers	whipped cream
Schmalz	lard
Schmarren	pancake cut up into small pieces
Schnecken	escargots
Schnittchen (Appe-tit)	canapé
Schnittlauch	chives
Schorle	wine and soda water mix
Schweinefleisch	pork
Schweinelendchen	small pieces of pork loin
Sekt	sparkling wine
Sellerie	celery
Semmel	bread roll
Senf	mustard
Sosse	gravy/sauce

Spanferkel
whole pig roasted over an open fire

Spargel
asparagus

Spätzle
spaetzle (type of pasta)

Speiseeis
ice-cream

Spinat
spinach

Steinpilz
type of mushroom (Boletus edulis)

Strammer Max
open sandwich of boiled ham and fried egg

Strudel
strudel

Süßspeise
sweet dish

Teig (in Öl gebacken)
pastry, batter (baked in oil)

Thunfisch
tuna

Tintenfisch
cuttlefish/squid

Topfen
soft curd cheese

Traube
grape

Truthahn
turkey

Tunke
sauce/gravy

Vesper
a break for eating/cold evening meal

Wachtel
quail

Wald-
forest

Walnuss
walnut

Wein (trocken/mild)
wine (dry/mild)

Wein (süss/Spätlese/Eiswein)
wine (sweet/late vintage/sweet wine made from grapes which have been exposed to frost)

Wein (Süsswein/Südwein)
wine (dessert wine/Mediterranean wine)

Weinbrand
brandy

Weisswurst
veal sausage

Wels
catfish

Würstchen
sausage

Zitrone
lemon

Zunge
tongue

Zwiebel
onion

5 On the road

5.1 Asking for directions

Excuse me, could I ask you something?	Verzeihung, dürfte ich Sie etwas fragen?	
	fair tsaioong, duerfter ikh zee etvass fragren?	
I've lost my way _____	Ich habe mich verlaufen/(with car)mich verfahren	
	ikh harber mikh fairlowfen/mikh fairfahren	
Is there a(n)... _____ around here?	Wissen Sie, wo hier in der Nähe ein(e)... ist?	
	vissen zee, vo heer in dayr nayher ain(er)... ist?	
Is this the way to...? ___	Ist dies die Strasse nach...?	
	ist dees dee shtrasser nakh...?	
Could you tell me _____ how to get to the... (name of place) by car/on foot?	Können Sie mir sagen, wie ich nach... (name of the place) fahren/gehen muss?	
	koenen zee meer zargen, vee ikh nakh ... fahren/gayhen muss?	
What's the quickest _____ way to...?	Wie komme ich am schnellsten nach...?	
	vee kommer ikh am shnellsten nakh...?	
How many kilometres __ is it to...?	Wieviel Kilometer sind es noch bis...?	
	veefeel kilomayter zint ez nokh biss...?	

geradeaus	überqueren	der Fluss
straight	cross	the river
nach links/links	die Kreuzung	die Brücke
abbiegen	the intersection	the bridge
left/turn left	die Strasse	die (Bahn)schranken
nach rechts/rechts	the street	the level crossing/the
abbiegen	die (Verkehrs)ampel	boomgates
right/turn right	the traffic light	das Schild
abbiegen	das Gebäude	Richtung...
turn	the building	the sign pointing to ...
folgen	an der Ecke	der Pfeil
follow	at the corner	the arrow

Ich weiss nicht, ich kenne mich hier nicht aus	I don't know, I don't know my way around here
Da sind Sie hier nicht richtig	You're going the wrong way
Sie müssen zurück nach...	You have to go back to...
Sie fahren über die...Strasse	You take...Street
Sie fahren über die...Strasse drüber	You cross over...Street
Da sehen Sie schon die Schilder	From there on you will see the signs
Da müssen Sie noch mal fragen	When you get there, you will have to ask again

Could you point it out on the map?	_____	Können Sie es mir auf der Karte zeigen?
		koennen zee ez meer owf dayr karter tsaigen?

5.2 Customs

● **Border documents:** along with your passport you must carry your original documents with you. These include your valid full driving licence (together with paper counterpart if photocard licence), vehicle registration document and motor insurance certificate. Contact your motor insurer for advice at least a month before taking your vehicle overseas to ensure that you are adequately covered. A warning triangle must be carried and a first-aid kit and a set of replacement bulbs are recommended.

There is no restriction on foreign currency. With the single European Market, travellers are only subject to selective spot checks. There is no restriction, either by quantity or value, on goods purchased by travellers from another EC country provided they are for their own personal use. However, guidelines have been published. As these are subject to change you are advised to contact your travel agent, customs or the Embassy for further details before travelling.

Ihren Pass bitte	Your passport, please
Die grüne Karte bitte	Your green card, please
Ihre Fahrzeugpapiere bitte	Your vehicle documents, please
Ihr Visum bitte	Your visa, please
Wohin fahren Sie?	Where are you heading?
Wie lange bleiben Sie/halten Sie sich dort auf?	How long are you planning to stay?
Haben Sie etwas zu verzollen?	Do you have anything to declare?
Würden Sie dies bitte öffnen?	Open this, please

My children are entered on this passport	Meine Kinder sind in diesem Pass eingetragen
	mainer kinder zint in deezem parss ain getrargen
I'm travelling through___	Ich bin auf der Durchreise
	ikh bin owf dayr doorkh raizer
I'm going on holiday to...	Ich fahre in den Urlaub nach...
	ikh fahrer in den oorlowp nakh...
I'm on a business trip ___	Ich bin auf Geschäftsreise
	ikh bin owf geshefts raizer
I don't know how long I'll be staying yet	Ich weiss noch nicht, wie lange ich bleibe
	ikh vaiss nokh nikht, vee langer ikh blaiber
I'll be staying here for a weekend	Ich bleibe hier übers Wochenende
	ikh blaiber heer uebers vokhen ender
– for a few days _____	Ich bleibe hier ein paar Tage
	ikh blaiber heer ain par targer
– for a week _____	Ich bleibe hier eine Woche
	ikh blaiber heer ainer vokher
– for two weeks _____	Ich bleibe hier zwei Wochen
	ikh blaiber heer tsvai vokhen
I've got nothing to declare	Ich habe nichts zu verzollen
	ikh harber nikhts tsoo fairtsollen

've got...with me _____	Ich habe ... mit
	ikh harber ... mit
- a carton of cigarettes _	Ich habe eine Stange Zigaretten
	ikh harber ainer shtanger tseegaretten
- a bottle of... _____	Ich habe eine Flasche...
	ikh harber ainer flusher...
- some souvenirs _____	Ich habe ein paar Andenken
	ikh harber ain par andenken
These are personal _____ effects	Das sind persönliche Sachen
	dass zint perzoenlikher zakhen
These are not new _____	Diese Sachen sind nicht neu
	deezer zakhen zint nikht noy
Here's the receipt _____	Hier ist der (Kassen)zettel
	heer ist dayr (kassen)tsettel
This is for private use _	Das ist für den eigenen Gebrauch
	dass ist fuer dayn aigenen gebrowkh
How much import duty _ do I have to pay?	Wieviel Einfuhrzoll muss ich zahlen?
	veefeel ainfoor tsoll muss ikh tsarlen?
Can I go now? _____	Darf ich jetzt gehen?
	darf ikh yetst gayhen?
Porter! _____	Gepäckträger!
	gepeck trayger!
Could you take this _____ luggage to...?	Würden Sie dieses Gepäck zu/in... bringen?
	vuerden zee deezes gepek tsoo/in... bringen?

5.3 Luggage

How much do I _____ owe you?	Wieviel bekommen Sie von mir?
	veefeel bekommen zee fon meer?
Where can I find a _____ luggage trolley?	Wo kann ich eine Gepäckkarre finden?
	vo kann ikh ainer gepek karrer finden?

Could you store this ____ luggage for me?	Kann ich dieses Gepäck zur Aufbewahrung abgeben?	
	kann ikh deezes gepek tsoor owfbevahrung apgayben?	
Where are the luggage ____ lockers?	Wo sind die Schliessfächer?	
	vo zint dee shleess fekher?	
I can't get the locker ____ open	Ich bekomme das Schliessfach nicht auf	
	ikh bekommer dass shleessfakh nikht owf	
How much is it per ____ item per day?	Wieviel kostet es je Stück pro Tag?	
	veefeel kostet es yay shtuek pro tark?	
This is not my bag/ ____ suitcase	Das ist nicht meine Tasche/mein Koffer	
	dass ist nikht mainer tasher/main koffer	
There's one item/bag/ ____ suitcase missing still	Es fehlt noch ein Stück/eine Tasche/ein Koffer	
	ez faylt nokh ain shtuek/ayner tasher/ain koffer	
My suitcase is_____ damaged	Mein Koffer ist beschädigt	
	main koffer ist beshaydikt	

5.4 Traffic signs

abbiegen	Autobahndreieck	Einfahrt
turn	motorway merging	entry/access
Anlieger frei	point	Ende der
residents only	Baustelle	Autobahn
Auffahrt	road works ahead	end of motorway
slip road/approach to	bei Nässe/Glätte	Frostaufbrüche
house	in wet -/icy	frost damage
Auflieger schwenkt	conditions	Gefahr
aus	Durchgangsverkehr	danger
trailer may swing	(verboten)	gefährlich
out	(no) throughway	dangerous
Ausfahrt	Einbahnstrasse	Gegenverkehr
exit	one way street	oncoming traffic

gesperrt (für alle Fahrzeuge)
closed (for all vehicles)
Glatteis
ice on road
Kurve(nreiche Strecke)
bend/dangerous bends
Licht einschalten/ ausschalten
switch on lights/end needs for lights
LKW
heavy goods vehicle
Naturschutzgebiet
nature reserve
Nebel
beware fog
Parkscheibe
parking disk
PKW
motorcar
Radfahrer kreuzen
cyclists crossing

Rasthof-stätte
services
Rastplatz bitte sauberhalten
please keep picnic area tidy
Rollsplit
loose chippings
Schleudergefahr
danger of skidding
Seitenstreifen nicht befahrbar
soft verges
Seitenwind
crosswind
Spurrillen
irregular road surface
Standstreifen
hard shoulder
Starkes Gefälle
steep hill
Stau
traffic jam
Stauwarnanlage
hazard lights

Steinschlag
falling stones
Talbrücke
bridge over a valley
Überholverbot
no overtaking
Umleitung
diversion
Unbeschränkter Bahnübergang
unguarded level crossing/dangerous crossing
Verengte Fahrbahn
narrow lane
Vorfahrt beachten
give way
Vorfahrtsstrasse
major road
Wasserschutzgebiet
protected reservoir area
zurückschalten
to change back

5.5 The car

Maximum speed for cars:
130km/h on motorways
100km/h outside built-up areas
50km/h in built-up areas
Give way: all traffic from the right has right of way, including slow
vehicles, except for major roads and other regulating traffic signs.
At roundabouts the traffic already on the roundabout has priority.

5.6 The petrol station

● **The petrol prices in Germany**, Austria and Switzerland are
comparable to those in the UK.

How many kilometres __ to the next petrol station, please?	Wieviel Kilometer sind es bis zur nächsten Tankstelle?
	veefeel kilomayter zint ez biss tsoor nexten tankshteller?
I would like...litres of..., _ please	Ich möchte ... Liter
	ikh moekhter ... liter
– super _____	Ich möchte ... Liter Super(benzin)
	ikh moehkter ... liter zooper(bentseen)
– leaded _____	Ich möchte ... Liter normal(es Bezin)
	ikh moehkter ... liter normarl(ez bentseen)
– unleaded_____	Ich möchte ... Liter bleifrei(es Benzin)
	ikh moekhter ... liter blaifrai(ez bentseen)
– diesel_____	Ich möchte ... Liter Diesel
	ikh moekhter ... liter deezel
I would like..._____ euros worth of petrol, please	Ich möchte für ... euros (Auto)gas
	ikh moekhter fuer ... euros (owto)gass

Fill her up, please_____	Voll bitte
	foll bitter
Could you check...?_____	Würden Sie bitte...kontrollieren?
	vuerden zee bitter...kontrolleeren?
– the oil level_____	Kontrollieren Sie bitte den Ölstand
	kontrolleeren zee bitter dayn oelshtant
– the tyre pressure_____	Kontrollieren Sie bitte den Reifendruck
	kontrolleeren zee bitter dayn raifendrukk
Could you change the___ oil, please?	Wechseln Sie bitte das Öl
	vekhseln zee bitter dass oel
Could you clean the ___ windows/the windscreen, please?	Reinigen Sie bitte die Windschutzscheibe
	rainigen zee bitter dee vint shoots shaiber
Could you give the_____ car a wash, please?	Kann ich hier mein Auto waschen lassen?
	kann ikh main owto heer vashen lassen?

5.7 Breakdown and repairs

I'm having car trouble. _ Could you give me a hand?	Ich habe eine Panne. Können Sie mir helfen?
	ikh harber ainer panner. koennen zee meer helfen?
I've run out of petrol ___	Ich habe kein Benzin mehr
	ikh harber kain bentseen mayr
I've locked the keys____ in the car	Ich habe die Schlüssel im Auto steckenlassen
	ikh harber dee shluessel im owto shtekken lassen
The car/motorbike/ ____ moped won't start	Das Auto/Motorrad/Moped springt nicht an
	dass owto/moator rat/moapet shprinkt nikht an
Could you contact the _ recovery service for me, please?	Könnten Sie für mich die Pannenhilfe benachrichtigen?
	koennten zee fuer mikh dee pannen hilfer benakh rikhtigen?

The parts of a car

battery	der Akku/die Batterie	*dayr akoo/batteree*
rear light	das Rücklicht	*dass ruekleekht*
rear-view mirror	der Rückspiegel	*dayr ruekshpeegell*
reversing light	der Rückfahrschein werfer	*dayr rueckfahrshaynverfer*
aerial	die Antenne	*dee antennar*
car radio	das Autoradio	*dass owtorardiyoo*
petrol tank	der Benzintank	*dayr bentseentank*
inside mirror	der Innenspiegel	*dayr innenshpeegel*
sparking plugs	die Zündkerze(n)	*dee tsuentkairtsen*
fuel filter/pump	das Treibstofffilter/ **die Triebstoff**pumpe	*dass traipshtofffilter/ dee traipshtoffpoomper*
wing mirror	der Aussenspiegel	*dayr owsenshpeegel*
bumper	die Stoßstange	*dee shtoass shtanger*
carburettor	der Vergaser	*dayr fairgarzer*
crankcase	das Kurbelgehäuse	*dass koorbellgehoyzer*
cylinder	der Zylinder	*dayr tsilinder*
ignition	die Zündung	*dee tsuendoong*
warning light	die Kontrollampe	*dee kontroal lamper*
dynamo	der Dynamo	*dayr deenamo*
accelerator	das Gaspedal	*dass gas pedarl*
handbrake	die Handbremse	*dee hantbremzer*
valve	das Ventil	*dass venteel*
silencer	der Auspufftopf	*dayr owspufftopf*
boot	der Kofferraum	*dayr kofferrowm*
headlight	der Scheinwerfer	*dayr shaynverfer*
crank shaft	die Kurbelwelle	*dee koorbelveller*
air filter	das Luftfilter	*dass looftfilter*
fog lamp	die Nebelleuchte	*dee naybel loykhter*
engine block	der Motorblock	*dayr moatorblock*
camshaft	die Nockenwelle	*dee nokkenveller*
oil filter/pump	das Ölfilter/ dieÖlpump	*dass oelfilter/dee oelpoomper*

dipstick	der Ölstandstab	*dayr oelshtuntshtarp*
pedal	das Pedal	*dass pedarl*
door	die Wagentür	*dee vargentuer*
radiator	der Kühler	*dayr kuehler*
brake disc	die Bremsscheibe	*dee bremzshayber*
spare wheel	das Ersatzrad	*dass erzatsrart*
indicator	der Blinker	*dayr blinker*
windscreen wiper	der Scheibenwischer	*dayr shaibenvisher*
shock absorbers	der Stossdämpfer	*dayr shtossdempfer*
sunroof	das Schiebdach	*dass sheebedakh*
spoiler	der Spoiler	*dayr shpoyler*
starter motor	der Startmotor	*dayr shtartmoator*
steering column	die Lenksäule	*dee lenkzoyler*
exhaust pipe	das Auspuffrohr	*dass owspoofrohr*
seat belt	der Sicherheitsgurt	*dayr zikherhaitsgoort*
fan	der Ventilator	*dayr venteelator*
distributor cables	das Verteilerkabel	*dass fertailerkarbel*
gear lever	der Schalthebel	*dayr shalt-haybel*
windscreen	die Windschutzscheibe	*dee vintshootsshaiber*
water pump	die Wasserpumpe	*dee vasserpoomper*
wheel	das Rad	*dass rart*
hubcap	die Radkappe	*dee rartkapper*
piston	der Kolben	*dayr kolben*

Could you call a _____ garage for me, please?	Könnten Sie für mich eine Werkstatt anrufen?
	koennten zee fuer mikh ainer vairkshtatt anroofen?
Could you give me_____ a lift to...?	Darf ich mit Ihnen nach...mitfahren?
	darf ikh mit eenen nakh...mitfahren?
– a garage/into town? __	Darf ich mit Ihnen bis zu einer Werkstatt/in die Stadt mitfahren?
	darf ikh mit eenen biss tsoo ainer verkshtatt/in dee shtatt mit fahren?
– a phone booth?_____	Darf ich mit Ihnen bis zu einer Telefonzelle mitfahren?
	darf ikh mit eenen biss tsoo ainer tellefoan tseller mit fahren?
– an emergency _____ phone?	Darf ich mit Ihnen bis zu einer Rufsäule mitfahren?
	darf ikh mit eenen biss tsoo ainer roofzoyler mit fahren?
Can we take my _____ bicycle/moped?	Kann mein Fahrrad/Moped auch mit?
	kann main fahr rat/moapet owkh mit?
Could you tow me to___ a garage?	Könnten Sie mich zu einer Werkstatt (ab)schleppen?
	koennten zee mikh tsoo ainer verkshtatt (ap)shleppen?
There's probably_____ something wrong with...(See pages 72–73)	Wahrscheinlich ist mit dem/der/den...etwas nicht in Ordnung
	varshainlikh ist mit daym/dayr/dayn...etvass nikht in ordnoong
Can you fix it? _____	Können Sie es reparieren?
	koennen zee es repareeren?
Could you fix my tyre? _	Können Sie den Reifen flicken?
	koennen zee dayn raifen flikken?
Could you change this _ wheel?	Können Sie das Rad wechseln?
	koennen zee dass rart vekhzeln?

Can you fix it so it'll get me to...?	Können Sie es soweit reparieren, dass ich damit nach ... fahren kann?
	koennen zee es zovait repareeren dass ikh darmit nakh ... fahren kann?
Which garage can help me?	Welche Werkstatt kann mir denn dann helfen?
	velkher verkshtatt kann meer denn dann helfen?
When will my car/bicycle be ready?	Wann ist mein Auto/Fahrrad fertig?
	vann ist main owto/fahr rart fairtikh?
Can I wait for it here?	Kann ich hier darauf warten?
	kann ikh heer darrowf varten?
How much will it cost?	Wieviel wird es kosten?
	veefeel virt es kosten?
Could you itemise the bill?	Können Sie die Rechnung spezifizieren?
	koennen zee dee rekhnoong shpetsi fitseeren?
Can I have a receipt for the insurance?	Ich hätte gern eine Quittung für die Versicherung
	ikh hetter gayrn ainer kvittoong fuer dee fairzikheroong

The parts of a bicycle

rear lamp	das Rücklicht	dass rueklikht
rear wheel	das Hinterrad	dass hinterrart
(luggage) carrier	der Gepäckträger	dayr gepektrayger
bicycle fork	das Steuer(kopf)rohr	dass shtoyerkopfrohr
bell	die Klingel	dee klingel
inner tube	der Schlauch	dayr shlowkh
tyre	der Reifen	dayr raifen
crank	die Kurbel	dee koorbel
gear change	der Umwerfer	dayr oomverfer
wire	das Kabel	dass karbel
dynamo	der Dynamo	dayr deenamo
bicycle trailer	der Fahrradanhänger	dayr fahrrartanhenger
frame	der Rahmen	dayr rarmen
dress guard	der Kleiderschutz	dayr klaidershoots
chain	die Kette	dee ketter
chain guard	der Kettenschutz	dayr kettenshoots
chain lock	das Kettenschloss	dass kettenshloss
milometer	der Kilometerzähler	dayr keelomaytertsayler
child's seat	der Kindersitz	dayr kinderzits
headlamp	der Scheinwerfer	dayr shainverfer
bulb	die Birne	dee beerner
pedal	das Pedal	dass pedarl
pump	die Pumpe	dee poomper
reflector	der Rückstrahler	dayr ruekshtrarler
break pad	die Bremsbacke	dee bremzbakker
brake cable	das Bremskabel	dass bremzkarbel
ring lock	das Sicherheitsschloss	dass zikherhaitsshloss
carrier straps	das Spannband	dass shpannbant
tachometer	der Tacho(meter)	dayr takhomayter
spoke	die Speiche	die shpaikher
mudguard	das Schutzblech	dass shootsblekh
handlebar	der Lenker	dayr lenker

chain wheel	das Zahnrad	*dass tsarnrart*
toe clip	der Rennhaken	*dayr renharken*
crank axle	die Tretwelle	*dee traytveller*
drum brake	die Trommelbremse	*dee trommelbremzer*
rim	die Felge	*dee felger*
valve	das Ventil	*dass venteel*
valve tube	der Ventilschlauch	*dayr venteelshlowkh*
gear cable	das Gangschaltungs-kabel	*dass gangshaltoongskarbel*
fork	die Vorderradgabel	*dee forderrartgarbel*
front wheel	das Vorderrad	*dass forderrart*
seat	der Sattel	*dayr zattel*

5.8 The bicycle/moped

● **Cycle paths** are common in towns and cities and their use is strongly recommended. Bikes can usually be hired at tourist centres. The maximum speed for mopeds is 40km/h both inside and outside town centres. Crash helmets are compulsory.

Ich habe keine Ersatzteile für Ihren Wagen/Ihr Fahrrad	I don't have parts for your car/bicycle
Ich muss die Ersatzteile irgendwo anders besorgen	I have to get the parts from somewhere else
Ich muss die Ersatzteile bestellen	I have to order the parts
Das dauert einen halben Tag	That'll take half a day
Das dauert einen Tag	That'll take a day
Das dauert ein paar Tage	That'll take a few days
Das dauert eine Woche	That'll take a week
Ihr Auto ist schrottreif	Your car is a write-off
Hier ist nichts mehr zu machen	It can't be repaired.
Das Auto/Motorrad/Moped/Fahrrad ist um...Uhr fertig	The car/motor bike/moped/bicycle will be ready at...o'clock.

5.9 Renting a vehicle

I'd like to rent a... _____	Ich möchte ein(en)...mieten *ikh moekhter ain(en)...meeten*
Do I need a (special) ___ licence for that?	Brauche ich dafür einen (bestimmten) Führerschein? *browkher ikh dafuer ainen (beshtimmten)* *fuehrershain?*
I'd like to rent the...for...	Ich möchte den/das...für...mieten *ikh moekhter dayn/dass...fuer...meeten*
- one day_____	Ich möchte den/das...für einen Tag mieten *ikh moekhter dayn/dass...fuer ainen tark* *meeten*
- two days _____	Ich möchte den/da ...für zwei Tage mieten *ikh moekhter dayn/dass...fuer tsvai targer* *meeten*
How much is that per ___ day/week?	Wieviel kostet das pro Tag/Woche? *veefeel kostet dass pro tark/vokher?*
How much is the _____ deposit?	Wie hoch ist die Kaution? *vee hokh ist dee kowtseeoan?*
Could I have a receipt___ for the deposit?	Geben Sie mir bitte eine Quittung, dass ich die Kaution bezahlt habe *gayben zee meer bitter ainer kvittoong,* *dass ikh dee kowtseeoan betsarlt harber*
How much is the _____ surcharge per kilometre?	Wie hoch ist der zusätzliche Kilometerpreis? *vee hokh ist dayr tsoo zetslikher kilo mayter* *praiss?*
Does that include_____ petrol?	Ist das Benzin mit enthalten? *ist dass bentseen mit enthalten?*
Does that include_____ insurance?	Ist die Versicherung mit enthalten? *ist dee fairsikhe roong mit enthalten?*
What time can I pick ___ the...up tomorrow?	Wann kann ich das...morgen abholen? *vann kann ikh dass...morgen apholen?*

When does the...have	Wann muss ich den/das...zurückbringen?
to be back?	*vann mooss ikh dayn/dass...tsooruekbringen?*
Where's the petrol tank?	Wo ist der Tank?
	vo ist dayr tank?
What sort of fuel does it take?	Was muss ich tanken?
	vass mooss ikh tanken?

5.10 Hitchhiking

Where are you heading?	Wohin fahren Sie?
	vohin fahren zee?
Can I come along?	Darf ich mit Ihnen mitfahren?
	darf ikh mit eenen mit fahren?
Can my boyfriend/ girlfriend come too?	Darf mein Freund/meine Freundin auch mit?
	darf main froynt/mainer froyndin owkh mitt?
I'm trying to get to...	Ich muss nach ...
	ikh mooss nakh ...
Is that on the way to...?	Liegt das auf dem Weg nach...
	leekt dass owf daym vayk nakh...
Could you drop me off...?	Könnten Sie mich absetzen?
	koennten zee mikh apsetsen?
– here?	Könnten Sie mich hier absetzen?
	koennten zee mikh heer apsetsen?
– at the...exit?	Könnten Sie mich an der Ausfahrt nach... absetzen?
	koennten zee mikh an dayr owsfahrt nakh... apsetsen?
– in the centre?	Könnten Sie mich im Zentrum absetzen?
	koennten zee mikh im tsentroom apsetsen?

English	German	Pronunciation
– at the next _____ roundabout?	Könnten Sie mich beim nächsten Kreisel/Kreisverkehr absetzen?	*koennten zee mikh baim nexten kraizel/krais fair kayr apzetsen?*
Could you stop here, ___ please?	Würden Sie bitte hier halten?	*vuerden zee bitter heer halten?*
I'd like to get out here __	Ich möchte hier raus	*ikh moekhter heer rows*
Thanks for the lift _____	Vielen Dank fürs Mitnehmen	*feelen dunk fuers mitnaymen*

6 Public transport

6.1 In general

● **Public transport** in Germany prides itself for being on time. Strikes (*Streiks*) are rare and only tend to occur around the trade unions' negotiations on pay which take place once a year. Tickets for buses can be bought as you get on the bus. Some unlimited travel cards/runabout tickets purchased for use on trains also cover all public means of transport within a designated area (*Verkehrsverbund*). Train tickets can be purchased either at the ticket office in the station or at ticket machines on the platforms.

Announcements

Der Zug nach...von...hat eine Verspätung von...Minuten	The train to...from has been delayed by...minutes.
Auf Gleis ... fährt ein der Zug nach.../aus...	The train now arriving at platform...is the train to.../from...
Auf Gleis...steht der Zug zur Abfahrt bereit nach...	The train to...is about to leave from platform...
Achtung! Bitte zurückbleiben! Ein Intercity fährt durch auf Gleis...	Attention please, keep your distance from the rail track, an intercity train will pass on platform...
Wir nähern uns (der Station/dem Hauptbahnhof)...	We're now approaching...(the station/ main station)

Where does this train go to?	Wohin fährt dieser Zug? *vohinn fairt deezer tsook?*
Does this boat go to...?	Fährt dieses Schiff nach ...? *fairt deezes shiff nakh...?*
Can I take this bus to...?	Kann ich mit diesem Bus nach...fahren? *kann ikh mitt deezem boos nakh...fahren?*

Does this train stop at...?	Hält dieser Zug in...?
	helt deezer tsook in...?
Is this seat taken/free/ reserved?	Ist dieser Platz besetzt/frei/reserviert?
	ist deezer plats bezetst/frai/rezerveert?
I've booked...	Ich habe ... reservieren lassen
	ikh haber ... rezerveeren lassen
Could you tell me where I have to get off for... ?	Könnten Sie mir sagen, wo ich aussteigen muss, um zu/zum/zur/zu den ... zu kommen?
	koennten zee meer zargen, vo ikh ows shtaigen mooss, oom tsoo/tsoom/tsoor/tsoo dayn ... tsoo kommen?
Could you let me know when we get to...?	Würden Sie mir bitte Bescheid sagen, wenn wir bei/beim/bei der/bei den ... sind?
	vuerden zee meer bitter beshait zargen, venn veer bai/baim/bai dayr/bai dayn ... zint?
Could you stop at the next stop, please?	Halten Sie bitte an der nächsten Haltestelle
	halten zee bitter an dayr nexten halter shteller
Where are we now?	Wo sind wir hier?
	vo zint veer heer?
Do I have to get off here?	Muss ich hier aussteigen?
	mooss ikh heer ows shtaigen?
Have we already passed...?	Sind wir schon an/am/an der ... vorbei?
	zint veer shoan an/am/an dayr ... forbai?
How long have I been asleep?	Wie lange habe ich geschlafen?
	vee langer harber ikh geshlarfen?
How long does... stop here?	Wie lange bleibt der/die ... hier stehen?
	vee langer blaipt dayr/dee ... heer shtayhen?
Can I come back on the same ticket?	Kann ich mit dieser Fahrkarte auch wieder zurück?
	kann ikh mit deezer farkarter owkh veeder tsooruek?

Can I change on this ___ ticket?	Kann ich mit dieser Fahrkarte umsteigen? *kann ikh mit deezer farkarter oom shtaigen?*
How long is this ticket___ valid for?	Wie lange ist diese Fahrkarte gültig? *vee langer ist deezer farkarter gueltikh?*
How much is the _____ supplement for the intercity?	Wie hoch ist der IC Zuschlag? *vee hokh ist der ee tsee tsooschlark?*

6.2 Questions to passengers

Ticket types

Erster oder zweiter Klasse?	First or second class?
Einfach oder hin und zurück/Hin- und Rückfahrt?	Single or return?
Raucher oder Nichtraucher?	Smoking or non-smoking?
Am Fenster oder am Gang?	Window or aisle?
Vorn oder hinten?	Front or back?
Sitzplatz oder Liegewagen?	Seat or couchette?
Oben, in der Mitte oder unten?	Top, middle or bottom?
Touristenklasse oder Business Class?	Tourist class or business class?
Kabine oder Sitzplatz?	Cabin or seat?
Einzel- oder Doppelkabine?	Single or double?
Zu wieviel Personen reisen Sie?	How many are travelling?

Destination

Wohin reisen Sie?	Where are you travelling?
Wann reisen Sie ab?	When are you leaving?
Abfahrt/(aircraft) Abflug um...	Your...leaves at...
Sie müssen in...umsteigen	You have to change trains at...
Sie müssen in...aussteigen	You have to get off at...
Sie müssen über...reisen	You have to travel via...
Die Hinreise fängt am...an	The outward journey is on...
Die Rückreise beginnt am...	The return journey is on...
Sie müssen spätestens...an Bord sein	You have to be on board by...

Inside the vehicle

Ihre Fahrkarte bitte	Your ticket, please
Ihre Reservierung bitte	Your reservation, please
Ihren (Reise)pass bitte	Your passport, please
Sie sitzen auf dem falschen Platz	You're in the wrong seat
Sie sitzen im/in der falschen...	You're on/in the wrong...
Dieser Platz ist reserviert	This seat is reserved
Sie müssen einen Zuschlag (be)zahlen	You'll have to pay a supplement
Der/die/das...hat eine Verspätung von ...Minuten	The...has been delayed by...minutes

6.3 Tickets

Where can I...?	Wo kann ich...?
	vo kann ikh...?
– buy a ticket?	Wo kann ich eine Karte kaufen?
	vo kann ikh ainer karter kowfen?
– make a reservation?	Wo kann ich einen Platz reservieren lassen?
	vo kann ikh ainen plats rezerveeren lassen?
– book a flight?	Wo kann ich einen Flug buchen?
	vo kann ikh ainen flook bookhen?
Could I have a...to..., please?	Ich möchte...nach...
	ikh moekhter...nakh...
– a single	Ich möchte einmal einfach nach...
	ikh moekhter ainmarl ainfakh nakh...
– a return	Ich möchte eine Rückfahrkarte nach...
	ikh moekhter ainer ruekfarkarter nakh...
first class	erster Klasse
	airster klasser
second class	zweiter Klasse
	tsvaiter klasser
tourist class	Touristenklasse
	tooristen klasser
business class	Business Class
	bizniss klarss
I'd like to book a seat/couchette/cabin	Ich möchte einen Sitzplatz/Liegewagenplatz/eine Kabine reservieren lassen
	ikh moekhter ainen zits plats/leeger vargen plats/ainer kabiner rezerveeren
I'd like to book a berth in the sleeping car	Ich möchte einen Platz im Schlafwagen reservieren lassen
	ikh moekhter ainen plats im shlarfvargen rezerveeren lassen
top/middle/bottom	oben/in der Mitte/unten
	oaben/in dayr mitter/oonten

smoking/no smoking ___	Raucher/Nichtraucher
	rowkher/nikht rowkher
by the window _____	am Fenster
	am fenster
single/double _____	Einzel-/Doppel-
	aintsel-/doppel-
at the front/back_____	vorn/hinten
	forn/hinten
There are...of us _____	Wir sind zu ...t (e.g. zweit, dritt, viert)
	veer zint tsoo ...t (e.g. tsvait, dritt, feert)
a car _____	ein Auto
	ain owto
a caravan_____	ein Wohnwagen
	ain voanvargen
...bicycles_____	...Fahrräder
	...fahr rayder
Do you also have...? ___	Haben Sie...?
	harben zee...?
– season tickets? _____	Haben Sie Sammelfahrscheine?
	harben zee zammel fahr shainer?
– weekly tickets? _____	Haben Sie Wochenkarten?
	harben zee vokhen karten?
– monthly season_____	Haben Sie Monatskarten?
tickets?	*harben zee moanarts karten?*
Where's? _____	Wo ist...?
	vo ist...?

6.4 Information

Where's the _____	Wo ist die Auskunft?
information desk?	*vo ist dee owskoonft?*
Where can I find a _____	Wo ist die Tafel mit den
timetable?	Abfahrtszeiten/Ankunftszeiten?
	vo ist dee tarfel mit den
	apfahrtstsaiten/ankunftstsaiten?

Where's the...desk?	Wo ist der Schalter für...? *vo ist dayr shalter fuer...?*
Do you have a city map with the bus/the underground routes on it?	Haben Sie einen Stadtplan mit dem Bus-/U-Bahnnetz? *harben zee ainen shtatplarn mit dem booss-/oobarn nets?*
Do you have a timetable?	Haben Sie einen Fahrplan? *harben zee ainen farplarn?*
I'd like to confirm/cancel/change my booking for/trip to...	Ich möchte meine Reservierung/Reise nach...bestätigen/annullieren/ändern *ikh moekhter mainer rezerveerung/raizer nakh ... beshtaytigen/annoo leeren/endern*
Will I get my money back?	Bekomme ich mein Geld zurück? *bekommer ikh main gelt tsooruek?*
I want to go to... How do I get there? (What's the quickest way there?)	Ich muss nach... Wie komme ich da (am schnellsten) hin? *ikh mooss nakh... vee kommer ikh da (am shnellsten) hin?*
How much is a single/return to...?	Wieviel kostet eine Fahrt/Rückfahrkarte nach...? *veefeel kostet ainer fart/ruek fahr karter nakh...?*
Do I have to pay a supplement?	Muss ich Zuschlag zahlen? *mooss ikh tsooshlak tsarlen?*
Can I interrupt my journey with this ticket?	Darf ich die Reise mit diesem Ticket unterbrechen? *darf ikh dee raizer mit deezem ticket oonter brekhen?*
How much luggage am I allowed?	Wieviel Gepäck darf ich mitnehmen? *veefeel gepeck darf ikh mitnaymen?*
Does this...travel direct?	Geht diese(r)/dieses ... direkt? *gayt deeze(r)/deezes ... direkt?*
Do I have to change? Where?	Muss ich umsteigen? Wo? *mooss ikh oom shtaigen? vo?*

Will there be any _____ stopovers?	Macht das Flugzeug eine Zwischenlandung?
	makht dass flooktsoyk ainer tsvishen landoong?
Does the boat call in at ___ any ports on the way?	Legt das Schiff unterwegs in irgendwelchen Häfen an?
	laykt dass shiff oontervegz in eergent velkhen hayfen an?
Does the train/ _____ bus stop at...?	Hält der Zug/Bus in...?
	helt der tsook/booss in...?
Where should I get off? ___	Wo muss ich aussteigen?
	vo mooss ikh ows shtaigen?
Is there a connection ___ to...?	Gibt es einen Anschluss nach...?
	gipt ez ainen anschluss nakh...?
How long do I have to ___ wait?	Wie lange muss ich warten?
	vee langer mooss ikh varten?
When does...leave? ____	Wann fährt...ab?
	vann fairt...ap?
What time does the ____ first/next/last...leave?	Wann fährt/(aircraft) fliegt der/die/das erste/nächste/letzte...?
	vann fairt/fleekt dayr/dee/dass airster/nexter/letster...?
How long does...take? _	Wie lange dauert die Fahrt/(flight) der Flug?
	vee langer dowert dee fahrt/dayr flook?
What time does...arrive _ in...?	Wann kommt...in...an?
	vann kommt...in...an?
Where does the...to... ___ leave from?	Wo fährt/(aircraft) fliegt der/die/das nach ...ab?
Is this...to...? _____	*vo fairt/fleekt dayr/dee/duss nakh...ap?*
	Ist dies ... nach...?
	ist deez ... nakh...?

6.5 Aeroplanes

● **On arrival** at a German airport (*Flughafen*), you will find the following signs:

Abflug	domestic/international	Ankunft
Inland/Ausland	departures	arrivals

After the check-in a boarding pass (*Bordkarte*, *Einsteigekarte*) is handed out which details the gate (*Flugsteig*) and departure time (*Abflugzeit*).

6.6 Trains

● **The rail network** is extensive. The Deutsche Bundesbahn is responsible for the national rail traffic. Generally there are four types of trains: *Intercity*, *Eilzug/Schnellzug* (fast train which does not stop at small stations - long distance), *S-Bahn* (designed to link smaller towns and villages on the outskirts with the city centre), *U-Bahn* (underground). A supplement is only to be paid for the *Intercity*. Seats can be reserved in advance on the *Intercity* and *Eilzug* only.

6.7 Taxis

● **In nearly all** large cities and bigger towns, there are plenty of taxis. Although German taxis have no fixed colour, they tend to be cream coloured. Virtually all taxis have a meter.

Besetzt	Taxistand	Frei
booked	for hire	taxi rank

Taxi!	_____	Taxi!
		tarksi!

Could you get me a ___ taxi, please?	Würden Sie mir bitte ein Taxi/eine Taxe bestellen?
	vuerden zee meer bitter ain tarksi/ainer tarkser beshtellen?
Where can I find a taxi _ around here?	Wo finde ich hier in der Nähe ein Taxi?
	vo finder ikh heer in dayr nayher ain tarksi?
Could you take me ___ to..., please?	Zu/zum/zur ... bitte
	tsoo/tsoom/tsoor ... bitter
– this address _____	Zu dieser Adresse bitte
	tsoo deezer adresser bitter
– the...hotel _____	Zum Hotel ... bitte
	tsoom hotel ... bitter
– the town/city centre _	Ins Zentrum bitte
	ins tsentroom bitter
– the station _____	Zum Bahnhof bitte
	tsoom barnhoaf bitter
– the airport_____	Zum Flughafen bitte
	tsoom flook harfen bitter
How much is the _____ trip to...?	Wieviel kostet die Fahrt zu/zum/zur...?
	veefeel kostet dee fart tsoo/tsoom/tsoor...?
How far is it to...?_____	Wie weit ist es nach ...?
	vee vait ist ez nakh ...?
Could you turn on the _ meter, please?	Würden Sie bitte das Taxameter einschalten?
	vuerden zee bitter dass taksarmeter ainshalten?
I'm in a hurry_____	Ich habe es eilig
	ikh haber ez ailikh
Could you speed _____ up/slow down a little?	Könnten Sie etwas schneller/langsamer fahren?
	koennten zee etvass shneller/langzarmer fahren?
Could you take a _____ different route?	Könnten Sie eine andere Strecke fahren?
	koennten zee ainer anderer shtrekker fahren?

'd like to get out here, please.	Lassen Sie mich hier aussteigen
	lassen zee mikh heer owsshtaigen
You have to go...here __	Sie müssen gehen...
	zee muessen gayhen...
You have to go straight on here.	hier geradeaus
	heer gerarder ows
You have to turn left here	hier (nach) links
	heer (nakh) links
You have to turn right here.	hier (nach) rechts
	heer (nakh) rekhts
This is it _____	Hier ist es
	heer ist ez
Could you wait a _____ minute for me, please?	Warten Sie bitte einen Augenblick
	varten zee bitter ainen owgenblick

7 Overnight accommodation

7.1 General

There is a great variety in overnight accommodation in Germany.
Hotels: the 'star-system' does not tend to be operational in Germany.
However, some are hotels *'vom ADAC empfohlen'* (recommended by
the German motoring organisation) promising good standard. Most
hotels offer *Halbpension* (half board) or *Vollpension* (full board).
Pension/Gasthof/Gästehaus: often smaller houses with B&B type
accommodation. A *Gasthof* would also have a restaurant.
Rasthof: accommodation available at motorway service stations.
Ferienwohnungen: holiday flats available in many tourist places,
recreational centres and/or camping sites.
Berghütten: mountain hut providing basic sleeping space.
Jugendherberge: Youth Hostels in Germany require an international
Youth Hostel pass and usually expect clients to provide their own
linen.
Campingplatz: free camping is not allowed in Germany. Camping
sites are usually privately run and not open all year round.

Wie lange bleiben Sie?	How long will you be staying?
Würden Sie bitte das Formular ausfüllen?	Fill out this form, please
Dürfte ich bitte Ihren Pass haben?	Could I see your passport?
Sie müssen eine Kaution stellen/zahlen	I'll need a deposit
Sie müssen im voraus (be)zahlen	You'll have to pay in advance

My name's...I've made a reservation over the phone/by mail	Mein Name ist...Ich habe einen Platz reservieren lassen (telefonisch/schriftlich)
	main narmer ist...ikh harber ainen plats rezerveeren lassen (telefoanish/shriftlikh)
How much is it per night/week/ month?	Wieviel kostet es pro Nacht/Woche/Monat?
	veefeel kostet ez pro nakht/vokher/moanart?
We'll be staying at least...nights/weeks	Wir bleiben mindestens...Nächte/Wochen
	veer blaiben mindestens...nekhter/vokhen
We don't know yet	Das wissen wir noch nicht genau
	dass vissen veer nokh nikht genow
Do you allow pets (cats/dogs)?	Sind Haustiere (Hunde/Katzen) erlaubt?
	zint howzteerer (hunder/katsen) erlowpt?
What time does the gate/door open/close?	Wann ist die Pforte/Tür geöffnet/(auf)/geschlossen/(zu)?
	van ist dee pforter/tuer geoeffnet/(owf)/geshlossen/(tsoo)?
Could you get me a taxi, please?	Würden Sie mir bitte ein Taxi bestellen?
	vuerden zee meer bitter ain tarksi beshtellen?
Is there any mail for me?	Ist Post für mich da?
	ist posst fuer mikh dar?

7.2 Camping

Where's the manager?	Wo ist der Verwalter?
	vo ist der fairvalter?
Are we allowed to camp here?	Dürfen wir hier campen?
	duerfen veer heer kampen?
There are...of us and ...tents	Wir sind ... Personen und haben ... Zelte
	veer zint ... perzoanen oont harben ... tselter

Sie können sich selbst einen Platz aussuchen	You can pick your own site
Sie bekommen einen Platz zugewiesen	You'll be allocated a site
Dies ist Ihre Platznummer	This is your site number.
Kleben Sie dies bitte auf Ihr Auto	Stick this on your car, please.
Sie dürfen diese Karte nicht verlieren	Please don't lose this card

Can we pick our _____ own site?
Dürfen wir selbst einen Platz aussuchen?
duerfen veer zelpst ainen plats ows zookhen?

Do you have a quiet ___ spot for us?
Haben Sie einen ruhigen Platz für uns?
harben zee ainen roohigen plats fuer oons?

Do you have any other _ sites available?
Haben Sie keinen anderen freien Platz?
harben zee kainen anderen fraien plats?

It's too windy/sunny/ ___ shady here.
Hier ist zuviel Wind/Sonne/Schatten
heer ist tsoofeel vint/zonner/shatten

It's too crowded here ___
Hier ist es zu voll
heer ist es tsoo foll

The ground's too _____ hard/uneven
Der Boden ist zu hart/ungleichmässig
der boaden ist tsoo hart/oon glaikh mayssikh

Do you have a level ___ spot for the camper/caravan/ folding caravan?
Haben Sie einen horizontalen Platz für das Wohnmobil/den Wohnwagen/Faltwagen?
harben zee ainen horitsontarlen plats fuer dass voan moabeel/dayn voanvargen/faltvargen?

Could we have _____ adjoining sites?
Können wir beieinander stehen?
koennen veer baiainander shtayhen?

Can we park the car ___ next to the tent?
Darf das Auto beim Zelt geparkt werden?
darf dass owto baim tselt geparkt verden?

How much is it per person/tent/caravan/car?	Was kostet es pro Person/Zelt/Wohnwagen/Auto?
	vass kostet ez pro perzoan/tselt/voanvargen/owto?
Are there any...?	Gibt es...?
	gipt ez...?
– any hot showers?	Warmwasserduschen?
	varm vasser dooshen?
– washing machines?	Waschmaschinen?
	wash masheenen?
Is there a...on the site?	Gibt es auf dem Gelände...?
	gipt ez owf daym gelender...?
Is there a children's play area on the site?	...einen Kinderspielplatz?
	...ainen kinder shpeel plats?
Are there covered cooking facilities on the site?	...eine überdachte Kochgelegenheit?
	...ainer ueber dakhter kokh gelaygen hait?
Can I rent a safe here?	Kann ich hier ein Schliessfach mieten?
	kann ikh heer ain shleesfakh meeten?
Are we allowed to barbecue here?	Darf man hier grillen?
	darf man heer grillen?
Are there any power points?	Gibt es Elektroanschlüsse?
	gipt ez elektro anshluesser?
When's the rubbish collected?	Wann wird der Abfall abgeholt?
	vann virt dayr apfal apgeholt?
Do you sell gas bottles (butane gas/propane gas)?	Verkaufen Sie Gasflaschen (Butangas/Propangas)?
	fairkowfen zee gassflashen (bootarn gass/proparn gass)?

7.3 Hotel/B&B/apartment/holiday house

| Do you have a single/double room available? | Haben Sie ein Einzelzimmer/Doppelzimmer frei? |
| | *harben zee ain aintsel tsimmer/doppel tsimmer frai?* |

per person/per room ___	Ist das einschliesslich

per person/per room ___ | pro Person/pro Zimmer
pro perzoan/pro tsimmer

Does that include____ | Ist das einschliesslich
breakfast/lunch/ | Frühstück/Mittagessen/Abendessen?
dinner? | *ist dass ainshleeslik frueh shtuek/mittark*
essen/arbent essen?

Could we have two ____ | Können wir zwei Zimmer nebeneinander
adjoining rooms? | bekommen?
koennen veer tsvai tsimmer nayben
ainander bekommen?

with/without_____ | Mit/ohne eigener Toilette/eigenem
toilet/bath/shower | Bad/eigener Dusche
mit/oaner aigener twaletter/aigenem
bart/aigener doosher

(not) facing the street __ | (nicht) an der Strassenseite
(nikht) an dayr shtrassen zaiter

with/without a view ____ | mit/ohne Seesicht
of the sea | *mit/oaner zayzikht*

Is there...in the hotel? __ | Gibt es im Hotel...?
gipt ez im hotel...?

Is there a lift in the ____ | Gibt es im Hotel einen Fahrstuhl?
hotel? | *gipt ez im hotel ainen fahrshtool?*

Do you have room ____ | Gibt es im Hotel Zimmerservice?
service? | *gipt ez im hotel tsimmer zairviss?*

Could I see the room? _ | Könnte ich das Zimmer mal sehen?
koennter ikh dass tsimmer marl zayhen?

Toilette und Dusche sind	You can find the toilet and
auf derselben Etage/in Ihrem	shower on the same floor/en
Zimmer	suite
Hier entlang bitte	This way, please
Ihr Zimmer ist im...Stock, die	Your room is on the...floor,
Nummer ist...	number...

Camping equipment

luggage space	das Gepäckapsis	dass gepekapsis
can opener	der Dosenöffner	dayr doazenoefner
butane gas bottle	die Butangasflasche	dee bootarn gasflasher
pannier	die Packtasche	dee pakktasher
gas cooker	der Gaskocher	dayr gasskokher
groundsheet	die Bodenplane	dee boadenplarner
mallet	der Hammer	dayr hammer
hammock	die Hängematte	dee hengermatter
jerry can	der Kanister	dayr kannister
campfire	das Lagerfeuer	dass largerfoyer
folding chair	der Klappstuhl	dayr klapshtool
insulated picnic box	die Kühltasche	dee kuehltasher
ice pack	das Kühlelemenz	dass kuehlelement
compass	der Kompass	dayr kompas
wick	der Glühstrumpf	dayr gluehshtroompf
corkscrew	der Korkenzieher	dayr korkentseeyer
airbed	die Luftmatratze	dee looftmatrattser
airbed plug pump	der Matratzenstöpsel	dayr matrattsenshtoepse
awning	das Vordach	dass fordakh
karimat	die Matte	dee matter

I'll take this room _____	Ich nehme dieses Zimmer	
	ikh naymer deezes tsimmer	
We don't like this one __	Dieses gefällt uns nicht	
	deezes gefellt oons nikht	
Do you have a larger/ __ less expensive room?	Haben Sie ein grösseres/billigeres Zimmer?	
	harben zee ain groesseres/billeegeres tsimmer?	
Could you put in_____ a cot?	Können Sie ein Kinderbett dazustellen?	
	koennen zee ain kinder bet datsoo shtellen?	

pan	die Pfanne	*dee pfanner*
pan handle	der Pfannenstiel	*dayr pfannenshteel*
primus stove	der Petroleumkocher	*dayr petroaleyoomkokher*
zip	der Reissverschluss	*dayr raissfershluss*
backpack	der Rucksack	*dayr rookzakk*
guy rope	die Zeltleine	*dee tseltlainer*
sleeping bag	der Schlafsack	*dayr shlarfzak*
storm lantern	die Sturmlaterne	*dee shtoormlaterner*
camp bed	die Liege	*dee leeger*
table	der Tisch	*dayr tish*
tent	das Zelt	*dass tselt*
tent peg	der Hering	*dayr hayring*
tent pole	die Zeltstange	*dee tseltshtanger*
vacuum flask	die Thermosflasche	*dee termowsflasher*
water bottle	die Feldflasche	*dee feltflasher*
clothes peg	die Wäscheklammer	*dee vesherklummer*
clothes line	die Wäscheleine	*dee vesherlainer*
windbreak	der Windschutz	*dayr vintshoots*
torch	die Taschenlampe	*dee tashenlamper*
pocket knife	das Taschenmesser	*dass tashenmesser*

What time's breakfast?	Ab wann gibt es Frühstück?
	ap vann gipt ez frueh shtuek?
Where's the dining room?	Wo ist der Speisesaal?
	vo ist dayr shpaize zarl?
Can I have breakfast in my room?	Kann ich Frühstück aufs Zimmer bekommen?
	kann ikh frueh shtuek owfs tsimmer bekommen?
Where's the emergency exit/fire escape?	Wo ist der Notausgang/die Feuertreppe?
	vo ist der noat owsgang/dee foyer trepper?

Where can I park my ___ car (safely)?	Wo kann ich mein Auto (sicher) abstellen?
	vo kann ikh main owto (zikher) apshtellen?
The key to room..., ___ please	Den Schlüssel für Zimmer...bitte
	dayn shluessel fuer tsimmer...bitter
Could you put this in ___ the safe, please?	Darf ich dies bitte in Ihren Safe legen?
	darf ikh dees bitter in eeren safe laygen?
Could you wake me ___ at...tomorrow?	Wecken Sie mich morgen bitte um...Uhr
	vekken zee mikh morgen bitter oom...ooer
Could you find a ___ babysitter for me?	Können Sie mir einen Babysitter besorgen?
	koennen zee meer ainen babysitter bezorgen?
Could I have an extra ___ blanket?	Würden Sie bitte eine extra Decke bringen?
	vuerden zee bitter ainer ekstrar dekker bringen?
What days do the ___ cleaners come in?	An welchen Tagen wird saubergemacht?
	an velkhen targen virt zowber gemakht?
When are the sheets/ ___ towels/tea towels changed?	Wann werden die Bettlaken/Handtücher/Geschirrtücher gewechselt?
	vann verden dee bett larken/hant tuekher/geshirr tuekher gevekhselt?

7.4 Complaints

We can't sleep for ___ the noise	Wir können durch den Lärm nicht schlafen
	veer koennen doorkh den lerm nikht shlarfen
Could you turn the ___ radio down, please?	Könnten Sie das Radio bitte etwas leiser stellen?
	koennten zee dass radeeo bitter etvass laizer shtellen?
We're out of toilet ___ paper	Das Toilettenpapier ist alle
	dass twaletten papeer ist aller

There aren't any.../ there's not enough...	Es gibt keine.../nicht genug... *es gipt kainer.../nikht genook ...*
The bed linen's dirty ___	Die Bettwäsche ist schmutzig *dee bettvesher ist shmootsikh*
The room hasn't been cleaned.	Das Zimmer ist nicht saubergemacht *dass tsimmer ist nikht zowber gemakht*
The kitchen is not clean	Die Küche ist nicht sauber *dee kuekher ist nikht zowber*
The kitchen utensils are dirty	Die Küchengeräte sind schmutzig *dee kuekhen gerayter zint shmootsikh*
The heater's not working	Die Heizung funktioniert nicht *dee haitsoong foonk tseeoneert nikht*
There's no (hot) water/electricity	Es gibt kein (warmes) Wasser/keinen Strom *ez gipt kain (varmez) vasser/kainen shtroam*
...is broken_____	... ist kaputt ... *ist kapoott*
Could you have that seen to?	Können Sie das in Ordnung bringen lassen? *koennen zee dass in ordnoong bringen lassen?*
Could I have another room/site?	Könnte ich ein anderes Zimmer/einen anderen Stellplatz bekommen? *koennter ikh ain underes tsimmer/ainen anderen stellplats bekommen?*
The bed creaks terribly _	Das Bett knarrt furchtbar *dass bet knarrt foorkhtbar*
The bed sags _____	Das Bett biegt sich durch *dass bet beekt zikh doorkh*
Could we have a board to put underneath?	Haben Sie ein Brett zum Drunterlegen? *harben zee ain bret tsoom droonter laygen?*
It's too noisy _____	Es ist zu laut *ez ist tsoo lowt*
We have trouble with bugs/insects	Wir haben Ärger mit Ungeziefer/Insekten *veer harben airger mit oongetseefer/ inzekten*

103

This place is full of mosquitoes	Es wimmelt hier von Mücken
	ez vimmelt heer fon mueken
– cockroaches	Es wimmelt hier von Kakerlaken
	ez vimmelt heer fon karker larken

7.5 Departure

See also 8.2 Settling the bill

I'm leaving tomorrow. Could I settle my bill, please?	Ich reise morgen ab. Könnte ich jetzt bitte abrechnen?
	ikh raizer morgen ap. koennter ikh yetst bitter aprekhnen?
What time should we vacate?	Wann müssen wir den/das/die... verlassen?
	vann muessen veer dayn/dass/dee... fairlassen?
Could I have my deposit/passport back, please?	Würden Sie mir bitte die Kaution/den Pass wiedergeben?
	vuerden zee meer bitter dee kowtseeoan/dayn pass veeder gayben?
We're in a terrible hurry	Wir haben grosse Eile
	veer harben groasser ailer
Could you forward my mail to this address?	Würden Sie mir bitte die Post an diese Adresse nachschicken?
	vuerden zee meer bitter dee posst an deezer adresser nakh shikken?
Could we leave our luggage here until we leave?	Dürfen wir unsere Koffer bis zur Abreise hier stehenlassen?
	duerfen veer oonzere koffer biss tsoor apraizer heer shtayen lassen?
Thanks for your hospitality	Vielen Dank für die Gastlichkeit/die Gastfreundschaft
	feelen dunk fuer dee gastlikh kait/dee gast froynt shaft

8

Money matters

● **In general,** banks are open to the public between 9am and 4.30pm. Some types of bank, smaller outlets and banks in smaller towns and villages often close for lunch between 12 noon and 2pm. Banks are closed on a Saturday. To exchange currency a proof of identity is usually required. The sign Geld/wechsel/ausländische Währung indicates that money can be changed. Hotels may also offer exchange facilities but at less favourable rates.

8.1 Banks

Where can I find a _____ bank/an exchange office around here?	Wo ist hier eine Bank/eine Wechselstube?
	vo ist heer ainer bank/ainer vekhsel shtoober?
Where can I cash this __ traveller's cheque/giro cheque?	Wo kann ich diesen Reisescheck/Postbarscheck einlösen?
	vo kann ikh deezen raizer shekk/postbar shekk ainloezen?
Can I cash this...here? _	Kann ich hier diesen ... einlösen?
	kann ikh heer deezen ... ainloezen?
Can I withdraw money _ on my credit card here?	Kann ich hier mit einer Kreditkarte Geld bekommen?
	kann ikh heer mit ainer kredit karter gelt bekommen?
What's the minimum/ __ maximum amount?	Was ist das Minimum/Maximum?
	vass ist dass minimoom/maksimoom?
Can I take out less_____ than that?	Darf ich auch weniger abheben?
	darf ikh owkh vayniger aphayben?
I've had some money __ transferred here. Has it arrived yet?	Ich habe Geld überweisen lassen. Ist es schon eingegangen?
	ikh harber gelt ueber vaizen lassen. ist ez shoan ain gegangen?
These are the details___ of my bank in the UK	Dies sind die Angaben von meiner Bank in England
	deez zint dee angarben fon mainer bank in englant

This is my bank/giro ___ number	Dies ist meine Kontonummer/ Gironummer
	deez ist mainer konto noomer/geero noomer
I'd like to change ___ some money	Ich möchte Geld wechseln
	ikh moekhter gelt vekhsein
- pounds into...___	- (englische) Pfund in...
	- _(englisher) pfoont in..._
- dollars into... ___	- Dollars in... - _(dollars) in..._
What's the exchange___ rate?	Wie hoch ist der Wechselkurs?
	vee hokh ist dayr vekhsel koors?
Could you give me___ some small change with it?	Können Sie mir auch etwas Kleingeld geben?
	koennen zee meer owkh etvass klaingelt gayben?
This is not right___	Das stimmt nicht
	dass shtimmt nikht

Unterschreiben Sie bitte hier	Sign here, please
Sie müssen dies ausfüllen	Fill this out, please
Darf ich bitte Ihren Pass haben?	Could I have your passport, please?
Darf ich Ihren Ausweis sehen?	Could I see some identification, please?
Darf ich Ihre Scheckkarte sehen?	Could I see your cheque guarantee card, please?

8.2 Settling the bill

| Could you put it on ___ my bill? | Könnten Sie das auf die Rechnung setzen? |
| | _koennten zee dass owf dee rekhnoong setsen?_ |

Does this amount include service?	Ist die Bedienung in diesem Betrag enthalten?
	ist dee bedeenoong in deezem betrark enthalten?
Can I pay by...?	Kann ich mit...bezahlen?
	kann ikh mit...betsarlen?
Can I pay by credit card?	Kann ich mit (einer) Kreditkarte bezahlen?
	kann ikh mit (ainer) kredit karter betsarlen?
Can I pay by traveller's cheque?	Kann ich mit einem Reisescheck bezahlen?
	kann ikh mit ainem raizer shekk betsarlen?
Can I pay with foreign currency?	Kann ich in ausländischer Währung bezahlen?
	kann ikh in owslendisher vayroong betsarlen?
You've given me too much/you haven't given me enough change	Sie haben mir zuviel/zuwenig (wieder)gegeben
	zee harben meer tsoofeel/tsoovaynikh (veeder) gegayben
Could you check this again, please?	Würden Sie das noch mal nachrechnen?
	vuerden zee dass nokh marl nakh rekhnen?
Could I have a receipt, please?	Ich hätte gern eine Quittung/den Kassenzettel
	ikh hetter gayrn ainer kvittoong/dayn kassen tsettel
I don't have enough money on me	Ich habe nicht genug Geld bei mir
	ikh harber nikht genook gelt bai meer
This is for you	Bitte, das ist für Sie
	bitter, dass ist fuer zee
Keep the change	Behalten Sie das Wechselgeld
	beharlten zee dass vekhselgelt

| Wir nehmen keine Kreditkarten/Reiseschecks/Auslands währungen an | We don't accept credit cards/traveller's cheques/foreign currency |

9

Post and telephone

9.1 Post

For giros, see 8 Money matters

● **Post offices** are open from Monday to Friday between 8.30am and 5pm. In smaller towns the post office closes at lunch. On Saturdays they are open until 12 noon. Stamps are only available at post offices and some hotel receptions. Post boxes are yellow.

Briefmarken stamps Päckchen/Pakete parcels	Postanweisung money orders	Telegramme telegrams

Where's...? _____	Wo ist...? *vo ist...?*
Where's the post office?	Wo ist hier ein Postamt? *vo ist heer ain postamt?*
Where's the main post office	Wo ist die Hauptpost? *vo ist dee howptpost?*
Where's the postbox? _	Wo ist hier ein Briefkasten? *vo ist heer ain breefkasten?*
Which counter should I go to...?	An welchem Schalter kann ich... ? *an velkhem shalter kann ikh...?*
– to send a fax _____	An welchem Schalter kann ich telefaxen? *an velkhem shalter kann ikh telefaksen?*
– to change money ____	An welchem Schalter kann ich Geld wechseln? *an velkhem shalter kann ikh gelt vekhseln?*
– to change giro cheques	An welchem Schalter kann ich Schecks einlösen? *an velkhem shalter kann ikh shekks ain loezen?*

– for a Telegraph Money Order?	An welchem Schalter kann ich telegrafisch Geld überweisen?
	an velkhem shalter kann ikh telegrarfish gelt ueber vaizen?
Poste restante	Postlagernd
	postlargernt
Is there any mail for me. My name's...	Ist Post für mich da? Mein Name ist...
	ist post fuer mikh dar? main narmer ist...

Stamps

What's the postage for a...to...?	Wieviel muss auf einen/ein(e)...nach...?
	veefeel mooss owf ainen/ain(er)...nakh...?
Are there enough stamps on it?	Sind genug Briefmarken drauf?
	zint genook breefmarken drowf?
I'd like... ...mark stamps	Ich möchte...Briefmarken zu...
	ikh moekhter...breefmarken tsoo...
I'd like to send this...	Ich möchte dies...schicken
	ikh moekhter dees...shikken
– express	Ich möchte dies per Eilboten schicken
	ikh moekhter dees payr ailboaten shikken
– by air mail	Ich möchte dies per Luftpost schicken
	ikh moekhter dees payr looftpost shikken
– by registered mail	Ich möchte dies per Einschreiben schicken
	ikh moekhter dees payr ainshraiben shikken

Telegram/fax

I'd like to send a telegram to...	Ich möchte ein Telegramm nach... aufgeben
	ikh moekhter ain telegram nakh... owfgayben
How much is that per word?	Wieviel kostet das pro Wort?
	veefeel kostet dass pro vort?
This is the text I want to send	Dies ist der Text des Telegramms
	dees ist dayr tekst dess telegrams

Shall I fill out the form __ myself?	Soll ich das Formular selbst ausfüllen?
	zoll ikh dass formoolar zelpst owsfuellen?
Can I make photocopies/_____ send a fax here?	Kann ich hier fotokopieren/telefaxen?
	kann ikh heer foto kopeeren/telefaksen?
How much is it _____ per page?	Wieviel kostet das pro Seite?
	veefeel kostet dass pro zaiter?

9.2 Telephone

See also 1.8 Telephone alphabet

● **All phone booths** offer a direct international service to the UK. To phone the UK dial 0044, plus the UK area code without the first 0. They are either coin phones or card phones. The cards can be bought at post offices. Some telephone booths will also accept credit cards. Phone booths do not accept incoming calls. A reverse-charge call (*ein R-Gespräch*) has to go via the operator. When phoning someone in Germany, you may be greeted with the subscriber's name or with *Hallo* or *Ja*.

Is there a phone box __ around here?	Ist hier eine Telefonzelle in der Nähe?
	ist heer ainer telefoan tseller in dayr nayher?
Could I use your_____ phone, please?	Dürfte ich Ihr Telefon benutzen?
	duerfter ikh eer telefoan benuetsen?
Do you have a _____ (city/region)...phone directory?	Haben Sie ein Telefonbuch (von der Stadt.../ dem Bezirk...)?
	harben zee ain telefoan bookh (fon dayr shtat.../daym betseerk...)?
Where can I get a_____ phone card?	Wo kann ich eine Telefonkarte kaufen?
	vo kann ikh ainer telefoan karter kowfen?
Could you give me...? __	Könnten Sie mir...geben?
	koennten zee meer...gayben?

– the number for_____ international directory enquiries	Könnten Sie mir die Nummer der Auslandsauskunft geben? *koennten zee meer dee noomer dayr owslantsowskoonft gayben?*
– the number of _____ room...	Könnten Sie mir die Nummer von Zimmer ... geben? *koennten zee meer dee noomer fon tsimmer ...gayben?*
– the international _____ access code	Könnten Sie mir die internationale Nummer geben? *koennten zee meer dee inter natseeo narle noommer gayben?*
– the country code for...	Könnten Sie mir die Ländervorwahl von ... geben? *koennten zee meer dee lender forvarl fon ... gayben?*
– the trunk code for... __	Könnten Sie mir die Vorwahl von ... geben? *koennten zee meer dee forvarl fon ... gayben?*
– the number of..._____	Könnten Sie mir die Rufnummer von ... geben? *koennten zee meer dee roofnoomer fon ... gayben?*
Could you check if this _ number's correct?	Könnten Sie kontrollieren, ob diese Nummer richtig ist? *koennten zee kontroleeren, op deezer noomer rikhtikh ist?*
Can I dial international _ direct?	Kann ich automatisch ins Ausland telefonieren? *kan ikh owtomatish ins owslant telefoaneeren?*
Do I have to go through the switchboard?	Muss ich über die Telefonistin telefonieren? *mooss ikh ueber dee telefoanisstin telefoaneeren?*

Do I have to dial '0' _____ first?	Muss ich erst eine Null wählen?
	mooss ikh erst ainer nool vaylen?
Do I have to book _____ my calls?	Muss ich ein Gespräch anmelden?
	mooss ikh ain geshprekh anmelden?
Could you dial this_____ number for me, please?	Würden Sie bitte folgende Nummer für mich anrufen?
	vuerden zee bitter folgender noommer fuer mikh anroofen?
Could you put me _____ through to.../extension..., please?	Verbinden Sie mich bitte mit.../Apparat...
	fairbinden zee mikh bitter mit.../apparart...
I'd like to place a _____ reverse-charge call to...	Ich möchte ein R-Gespräch mit...
	ikh moekhter ain air-geshprekh mit...
What's the charge per __ minute?	Wieviel kostet das pro Minute?
	veefeel kostet dass pro meenooter?
Have there been any ___ calls for me?	Hat jemand für mich angerufen?
	hat yaymant fuer mikh angeroofen?

The conversation

Hello, this is... _____	Guten Tag, ... hier
	gooten tark, ... heer
Who is this, please? ___	Mit wem spreche ich?
	mit vaym shprekher ikh?
Is this...? _____	Spreche ich mit...?
	shprekher ikh mit...?
I'm sorry, I've dialled ___ the wrong number	Entschuldigung, ich habe mich verwählt
	ent shool digung, ikh harber mikh fairvaylt
I can't hear you_____	Ich kann Sie nicht verstehen
	ikh kann zee nikht fairshtayhen
I'd like to speak to... ___	Ich möchte ... sprechen
	ikh moekhter ... shprekhen
Extension..., please ____	Apparat ... bitte
	apparart ... bitter

Could you ask him/her _ to call me back?

Er/sie möchte mich bitte zurückrufen
ayr/zee moekhter mikh bitter tsooruekh roofen

My name's... _____
My number's...

Mein Name ist... Meine Nummer ist...
main narmer ist... mainer noommer ist...

I'll call back tomorrow__

Ich rufe ihn/sie morgen wieder an
ikh roofer een/zee morgen veeder an

Telefon für Sie	There's a phone call for you
Sie müssen erst eine Null wählen	You have to dial '0' first
(Einen) Augenblick bitte	One moment, please
Es antwortet niemand	There's no answer
Die Nummer ist besetzt	The line's engaged
Wollen Sie warten?	Do you want to hold?
Ich verbinde	Putting you through
Sie haben die falsche Nummer (gewählt)	You've got a wrong number
Er/sie ist im Augenblick nicht da/im Haus	He's/she's not here right now
Er/sie ist...wieder zu erreichen	He'll/she'll be back...
Dies ist der Anrufbeantworter von...	This is the answering machine of...

10 Shopping

● **Opening times:** Supermarkets and department stores are open Monday to Friday 8.30/9am–5.30/6pm, on Saturdays they are usually closed after 2pm. However, every first Saturday of the month is a *langer Samstag* (long Saturday) which means that shops stay open until about 6pm. In many larger towns shops stay open until 8.30pm on a Thursday. Smaller shops may close for lunch between 12 noon and 2pm and on Wednesday afternoons.

10.1 Shopping conversations

Where can I get...?	In welchem Geschäft kann ich ... bekommen?
	in velkhem gesheft kan ikh ... bekommen?
When does this shop open?	Wann hat dieses Geschäft geöffnet?
	van hat deezez gesheft geoeffnet?
Could you tell me where the...department is?	Können Sie mir sagen, wo die ... Abteilung ist?
	koennen zee meer zargen vo dee ... aptailoong ist?
Could you help me, please? I'm looking for...	Können Sie mir bitte helfen? Ich suche...
	koennen zee meer bitter helfen? ikh zookher...
Do you sell English/ American newspapers?	Verkaufen Sie englische/amerikanische Zeitungen?
	fairkowfen zee englisher/amerikarnisher tsai toongen?

Werden Sie schon bedient?	Are you being served?

No, I'd like...	Nein, ich möchte...
	nain, ikh moekhter...
I'm just looking, if that's all right	Ich möchte mich nur mal umsehen
	ikh moekhter mikh noor marl oom zayhen

Andenkenladen
souvenir shop

Antiquitäten antiques

Bäckerei
bakery

Beleuchtung
lighting

Buchhandlung
bookshop

Drogerie chemist

Einkaufszentrum
shopping centre

Eisenwarengeschäft
hardware store

Elektrogeräte
electrical appliances

Fahrradgeschäft
cycle shop

Feinkost
delicatessen

Fischgeschäft
fishmonger

Flohmarkt
fleamarket

Florist
florist

Frisör
hairdresser

Gärtnerei
nursery

Geschäft shop

Getränkemarkt
drinks store

Handarbeitsgeschäft
needlework and wool
 shop

Handlung
dealer

Haushaltswaren
household goods

Heimwerker Markt
DIY-store

Kaufhaus
department store

Konditorei
cake shop

Kosmetiksalon
beauty parlour

Kürschner
furrier

Kurzwarenhandlung
haberdashery

Laden
shop

Metzgerei
butcher's

Molkereigeschäft
dairy

Münzwäscherei
laundrette

Musikalienhandlung
music shop

Obst und Gemüse
greengrocer

Ökoladen
health food shop

Optiker
opticians

Pelze
fur

Rauchwarengeschäft
tobacconist

Raumausstat-
 tung(shaus)
interior decorator

Reinigung
dry cleaner

Schallplatten-
 geschäft
record shop

Schlachter butcher

Schmuck
jeweller

Schuhgeschäft
shoe shop

Schuhmacher/
 Schuster
cobbler

Second-Hand-Laden
second-hand goods

Spielzeuggeschäft
toy shop

Spirituosenhandlung
off licence

Sportartikel
sports shop

Süsswaren
sweet shop

Tante-Emma-Laden
corner shop

Trafik
tobacconist

Uhrengeschäft
clock shop/jeweller

Wäscherei
laundry

Zoohandlung
pet shop

Sonst noch (et)was?	**Anything else?**

Yes, I'd also like...	Ja, bitte auch noch...
	yar, bitter owkh nokh...
No, thank you. That's all	Nein, danke. Das ist alles
	nain, dunker. dass ist alles
Could you show me...?	Können Sie mir ... zeigen?
	koennen zee meer ... tsaigen?
I'd prefer...	Ich möchte lieber...
	ikh moekhter leeber...
This is not what I'm looking for	Das ist nicht, was ich suche
	dass ist nikht vass ikh zookher
I'll keep looking	Ich sehe mich erst noch mal weiter um
	ikh zayher mikh airst nokh marl vaiter oom
Do you have something...?	Haben Sie nicht etwas, was...ist?
	harben zee nikht etvass, vass...ist?
– less expensive?	Haben Sie nicht etwas Billigeres?
	harben zee nikht etvass billigerez?
– something smaller?	Haben Sie nicht etwas Kleineres?
	harben zee nikht etvass klainerez?
– something larger?	Haben Sie nicht etwas Grösseres?
	harben zee nikht etvass groerserez?
I'll take this one	Ich nehme dies
	ikh naymer deez
Does it come with instructions?	Ist eine Gebrauchsanweisung dabei?
	ist ainer gebrowkhs anvai zoong darbai?
It's too expensive	Ich finde es zu teuer
	ikh finder ez tsoo toyer
I'll give you...	Ich biete Ihnen...
	ikh beeter eenen...
Could you keep this for me? I'll come back for it later	Kann ich ihn/sie/es hierlassen? Ich hole ihn/sie/es nachher ab
	kan ikh een/zee/es heerlassen? ikh hoaler een/zee/es nakhherr ap

Have you got a bag____ for me, please?	Haben Sie bitte eine Tüte für mich?
	harben zee bitter ainer tueter fuer mikh?
Could you giftwrap ____ it, please?	Könnten Sie es bitte in Geschenkpapier einpacken?
	koennten zee ez bitter in geshenk papeer ainpakken?

(Es) tut mir leid, das haben/führen wir nicht	I'm sorry, we don't have that
(Es) tut mir leid, das ist ausverkauft	I'm sorry, we're sold out
Tut mir leid, das kriegen wir erst... wieder rein	I'm sorry, that won't be in until...
Sie können an der Kasse zahlen	You can pay at the cash desk
Wir nehmen keine Kreditkarten an	We don't accept credit cards
Wir nehmen keine Reiseschecks an	We don't accept traveller's cheques
Wir nehmen kein ausländisches Geld/keine Fremdwährungen an	We don't accept foreign currency

10.2 Food

I'd like a hundred ____ grams of..., please	Hundert Gramm...bitte
	hoondert gramm...bitter
– five hundred grams/ ____ half a kilo of...	Fünfhundert Gramm/ein halbes Kilo/(ein Pfund) ... bitte
	fuenfhoondert gramm/ain halbes keelo/(ain pfoont)...bitter
– a kilo of... ____	Ein Kilo ... bitte *ain keelo...bitter*
Could you...it for me,____ please?	Würden Sie es mir bitte...?
	vuerden zee es meer bitter...?

Could you slice it/ dice it for me, please?	Würden Sie es mir bitte in Scheiben/Stücke/(kleine)Würfel schneiden? *vuerden zee es meer bitter in shaiben/shtueker/(klainer) vuerfel shnaiden?*
Could you grate it for me, please?	Würden Sie es mir bitte reiben? *vuerden zee es meer bitter raiben?*
Can I order it?	Kann ich es bestellen? *kan ikh es beshtellen?*
I'll pick it up tomorrow/ at...	Ich hole es morgen/um...Uhr ab *ikh hoaler es morgen/oom...oor ap*
Can you eat/drink this?	Kann man das essen/trinken? *kan man dass essen/trinken?*
What's in it?	Woraus besteht es? *vorows beshtayt es?*

10.3 Clothing and shoes

I saw something in the window. Shall I point it out?	Ich habe im Schaufenster etwas gesehen. Soll ich es Ihnen zeigen? *ikh harber im showfenster etvass gesayhen. zoll ikh ez eenen tsaigen?*
I'd like something to go with this	Ich möchte gern etwas, was hierzu passt *ikh moekhter gayrn etvass, vass heertsoo passt*
Do you have shoes to match this colour?	Haben Sie Schuhe in derselben Farbe wie diese hier? *harben zee shooer in derselben farber vee deezer heer?*
I'm a size...in the UK	In England habe ich Grösse... *in englant harber ikh groesser...*
Can I try this on?	Darf ich dies anprobieren? *darf ikh dees anprobeeren?*

Where's the fitting _____ room?	Wo ist die Anprobe? *vo ist dee anprober?*
It doesn't fit _____	Es passt mir nicht *es passt meer nikht*
This is the right size _____	Das ist die richtige Grösse *dass ist dee rikhtiger groesser*
It doesn't suit me _____	Es steht mir nicht *es shtayt meer nikht*
Do you have this/ _____ these in...?	Haben Sie dies/diese auch in...? *harben zee dees/deezer owkh in...?*
The heel's too high/low _	Ich finde den Absatz zu hoch/niedrig *ikh finder den apzats tsoo hokh/needrikh*
Is this/are these _____ genuine leather?	Ist dies/sind diese aus echtem Leder? *ist dees/zint deezer ows ekhtem layder?*
I'm looking for a... _____ for a...-year-old baby/child	Ich suche ein(en)/eine ... für ein Baby/Kind von ... Jahren *ikh zookher ain(en)/ainer ... fuer ain baby/kint fon ... yahren*
I'd like a... _____	Ich hätte gern ein(en)/eine ... aus *ikh hetter gayrn ain(en)/ainer ... ows*
– silk _____	Ich hätte gern ein(en)/eine ... aus Seide *ikh hetter gayrn ain(en)/ainer ... ows zaider*
– cotton _____	Ich hätte gern ein(en)/eine ... aus Baumwolle *ikh hetter gayrn ain(en)/ainer ... ows bowmvoller*
– woollen _____	Ich hätte gern ein(en)/eine ... aus Wolle *ikh hetter gayrn ain(en)/ainer ... ows voller*
– linen _____	Ich hätte gern ein(en)/eine ... aus Leinen *ikh hetter gayrn ain(en)/ainer ... ows lainen*

Chemisch reinigen	Maschinenwaschbar	Nicht bügeln
Dry clean	Machine washable	Do not iron
Handwäsche	Nass aufhängen	Nicht schleudern
Hand wash	Drip dry	Do not spin

What temperature can I wash it at?	Bei welcher Temperatur kann ich es waschen?
	bai velkher temperatoor kan ikh es vashen?
Will it shrink in the wash?	Läuft es (in der Wäsche) ein?
	loyft es (in der wesher) ain?

At the cobbler

Could you mend these shoes?	Können Sie diese Schuhe reparieren?
	koennen zee deezer shooer repareeren?
Could you put new soles/heels on these?	Können Sie diese hier versohlen/die Absätze erneuern?
	koennen zee deezer heer fairzoalen/dee apsetzer ernoyern?
When will they be ready?	Wann sind sie fertig?
	vann zint zee fairtikh?
I'd like..., please	Ich möchte (gern)...
	ikh moekhter (gayrn)...
– a tin of shoe polish	Ich möchte gern eine Dose Schuhcreme
	ikh moekhter gayrn ainer doazer shookremer
– a pair of shoelaces	Ich möchte gern ein Paar Schuhbänder
	ikh moekhter gayrn ain par shoobender

10.4 Photographs and video

I'd like a film for this camera, please	Ich möchte einen Film für diesen Apparat
	ikh moekhter ainen film fuer deezen apparart
– a cartridge	Ich möchte eine Cassette
	ikh moekhter ainer kassetter
– a one twenty-six cartridge	Ich möchte eine 126er Cassette
	ikh moekhter ainer ain hoondert zekhs oont tvantsiger kassetter

– a slide film _____ Ich möchte einen Diafilm
ikh moekhter ainen diafilm

– a film cartridge _____ Ich möchte eine Filmcassette
ikh moekhter ainer filmkassetter

– a videotape _____ Ich möchte ein Videoband
ikh moekhter ain veedeeo bant

colour/black and white _ Farbe/schwarzweiss
farber/shvarts vaiss

super eight _____ Super 8
zooper akht

12/24/36 exposures____ 12/24/36 Aufnahmen
*tsvoelf/feer oont tsvantsikh/zekhs oont
draissikh owfnarmen*

ASA/DIN number _____ ISO Wert
eessoh vayrt

daylight film_____ (der) Tageslichtfilm
(dayr) targes likht film

film for artificial light ___ (der) Kunstlichtfilm
(dayr) koonst likht film

Problems

Could you load the ____ Würden Sie den Film bitte für mich
film for me, please? einlegen?
*vuerden zee den film bitter fuer mikh
ainlaygen?*

Could you take the film_ Würden Sie bitte den Film für mich aus
out for me, please? der Kamera nehmen?
*vuerden zee bitter dayn film fuer mikh ows
der kamerar naymen?*

Should I replace _____ Muss ich die Batterien auswechseln?
the batteries? *mooss ikh dee battereeyen ows vekhseln?*

Could you have a look _ Könnten Sie sich bitte mal die Kamera
at my camera, please? ansehen? Sie funktioniert nicht mehr
It's not working *koennten zee zikh bitter marl dee kamerar
anzayhen? zee foonk tseeoneert nikht
mair*

English	German
The...is broken	Der/die/das ... ist kaputt
	dayr/dee/dass ... ist kapoott
The film's jammed	Der Film klemmt
	dayr film klemmt
The film's broken	Der Film ist gerissen
	dayr film ist gerissen
The flash isn't working	Das Blitzlicht funktioniert nicht
	dass blits likht foonk tseeoneert nikht
I'd like to have this film developed/printed, please	Ich möchte diesen Film entwickeln/abziehen lassen
	ikh moekhter deezen film entvikkeln/ap tseeyen lassen
I'd like...prints from each negative	Ich möchte von jedem Negativ ... Abzüge
	ikh moekhter fon yaydem negateef ... aptsueger
glossy/mat	glänzend/matt
	glentsent/mat
7x5	Sieben mal fünf
	zeeben marl fuenf
I'd like to reorder these photos	Ich möchte diese Fotos nachbestellen
	ikh moekhter deezer fotos nakh beshtellen
I'd like to have this photo enlarged	Ich möchte dieses Foto vergrössern lassen
	ikh moekhter deezez foto fair groessern lassen
How much is processing?	Wieviel kostet das Entwickeln?
	veefeel kostet dass entvikkeln?
– printing	Wieviel kosten die Abzüge?
	veefeel kosten dee aptsueger?
– it to reorder	Wieviel kostet die Nachbestellung?
	veefeel kostet dee nakh beshtelloong?
– the enlargement	Wieviel kostet die Vergrösserung?
	veefeel kostet dee fair groesseroong?
When will they be ready?	Wann sind sie fertig?
	vann zint zee fairtikh?

10.5 At the hairdresser's

English	German
Do I have to make an __ appointment?	Muss ich einen Termin machen? *mooss ikh ainen termeen makhen?*
Can I come in straight__ away?	Kann ich sofort drankommen? *kann ikh zofort drannkommen?*
How long will I have ___ to wait?	Wie lange muss ich warten? *vee langer mooss ikh varten?*
I'd like a shampoo/ ____ haircut	Ich möchte mir die Haare waschen/schneiden lassen *ikh moekhter meer dee haarer vashen/shnaiden lassen*
I'd like a shampoo for __ oily/dry hair, please	Ein Shampoo gegen fettes/trockenes Haar bitte *ain shampoo gaygen fettez/trokkenez haar bitter*
an anti-dandruff _____ shampoo	Ein Shampoo gegen Schuppen bitte *ain shampoo gaygen shooppen bitter*
– a shampoo for_____ permed/coloured hair	Ein Shampoo für dauergewelltes/gefärbtes Haar bitte *ain shampoo fuer dower gevelltes/gefayrptes har bitter*
– a colour rinse_____ shampoo	Ein Farbshampoo bitte *ain farp shampoo bitter*
– a shampoo with _____ conditioner	Ein Shampoo mit einem Pflegemittel bitte *ain shampoo mit ainem pflayger mittel bitter*
– highlights _____	Blonde Strähnchen bitte *blonder shtraynkhen bitter*
Do you have a colour __ chart, please?	Hätten Sie eine Farbenkarte? *hetten zee ainer farben karter?*
I want to keep it the____ same colour	Ich möchte die Farbe behalten *ikh moekhter dee farber behalten*
I'd like it darker/lighter _	Ich möchte es dunkler/heller haben *ikh moekhter ez doonkler/heller harben*

I'd like/I don't want ___ hairspray	Ich möchte (keinen) Haarfestiger *ikh moekhter (kainen) haarfestigger*
- gel _____	Ich möchte (kein) Gel *ikh moekhter (kain) jell*
- lotion _____	Ich möchte (keine) Lotion *ikh moekhter (kainer) loatseeyoan*
I'd like a short fringe ___	Ich möchte meinen Pony kurz tragen *ikh moekhter mainen pony koorts tragen*
Not too short at the ___ back	Hinten nicht zu kurz schneiden bitte *hinten nikht tsoo koorts shnaiden bitter*
Not too long here _____	Hier bitte nicht zu lang *heer bitter nikht tsoo lang*
I'd like/I don't want ___ (many) curls	Ich möchte (nicht zuviel) Locken *ikh moekhter (nikht tsoofeel) locken*
It needs a little/_____ a lot taken off	Bitte schneiden Sie ein kleines bisschen/ein gutes Stück ab *bitter shnaiden zee ain klainez bisskhen/ain gootez shtook ap*
I'd like it the same ___ as in this photo	Ich möchte eine Frisur wie auf diesem Foto *ikh moekhter ainer frizoor vee owf deezem foto*
Could you put the ___ drier up/down a bit?	Könnten Sie die Haube etwas höher/niedriger einstellen? *koennten zee dee howber etvass hoeher/needriger ain shtellen?*
I'd like a facial_____	Ich möchte eine Gesichtsmaske *ikh moekhter ainer gezikhts masker*
- a manicure _____	Ich möchte mich maniküren lassen *ikh moekhter mikh manni kueren lassen*
- a massage _____	Ich möchte eine Massage *ikh moekhter ainer massarjer*

Welchen Schnitt möchten Sie?	How do you want it cut?
Welches Modell möchten Sie?	What style did you have in mind?
Welche Farbe soll es sein?	What colour did you want it?
Ist das die richtige Temperatur?	Is the temperature all right for you?
Wünschen Sie etwas zu(m) Lesen?	Would you like something to read?
Wünschen Sie etwas zu trinken?	Would you like a drink?
Ist es so richtig?	Is this what you had in mind?

Could you trim _____ my fringe?	Würden Sie mir bitte den Pony kürzen? *vuerden zee meer bitter dayn pony kuertsen?*
my beard/ _____ my moustache?	Würden Sie mir bitte den Bart/Schnurrbart stutzen? *vuerden zee meer bitter dayn bart/shnoorbart shtootsen?*
I'd like a shave, please _	Rasieren bitte *razeeren bitter*
I'd like a wet shave, _____ please	Ich möchte bitte nass rasiert werden *ikh moekhter bitter nass razeert verden*

11

At the Tourist Information Centre

11.1 Places of interest

Where's the Tourist ____ Information, please?	Wo ist der Fremdenverkehrsverein? *vo ist dayr fremden fayr kayrs fairrain?*
Do you have a city ____ map?	Haben Sie einen Stadtplan? *harben zee ainen shtatplan?*
Could you give me ____ some information about...?	Können Sie mir Auskunft geben über...? *koennen zee meer owskoonft gayben ueber...?*
How much is that? ____	Wieviel kostet das? *veefeel kostet dass?*
What are the main ____ places of interest?	Welches sind die wichtigsten Sehenswürdigkeiten? *velkhez zint dee vikhtikhsten zayhens vuerdikh kaiten?*
Could you point them ____ out on the map?	Könnten Sie mir die auf dem Plan zeigen? *koennten zee meer dee owf daym plarn tsaigen?*
What do you ____ recommend?	Was empfehlen Sie uns? *vass empfaylen zee oons?*
We'll be here for a ____ few hours	Wir bleiben hier ein paar Stunden *veer blaiben heer ain par shtoonden*
– a day ____	Wir bleiben hier einen Tag *veer blaiben heer ainen tark*
– a week ____	Wir bleiben hier eine Woche *veer blaiben heer ainer vokher*
We're interested in... ____	Wir interessieren uns für... *veer interesseeren oons fuer...*
Is there a scenic walk ____ around the city?	Können wir einen Stadtrundgang machen? *koennen veer ainen shtat roont gang makhen?*
How long does it take? ____	Wie lange dauert der? *vee langer dowert dayr?*

Where does it _____ start/end?	Wo ist der Anfang/das Ende? *vo ist der anfang/dass ender?*
Are there any boat _____ cruises here?	Gibt es hier Rundfahrtboote/-schiffe/Ausflugsschiffe? *gipt es heer roont fahrt boater/shiffer/-ows flooks shiffer?*
Where can we board? __	Wo können wir an Bord gehen? *vo koennen veer an bort gayhen?*
Are there any bus_____ tours?	Gibt es Busrundfahrten? *gipt es boos roont fahrten?*
Where do we get on? __	Wo müssen wir einsteigen? *vo muessen veer ainshtaigen?*
Is there a guide who __ speaks English?	Gibt es einen englisch sprechenden Führer? *gipt ez ainen english shprekhenden fuerer?*
Are there any_____ excursions?	Gibt es Ausflüge? *gipt ez owsflueger?*
What trips can we take _ around the area?	Welche Ausflüge in die Umgebung kann man machen? *velkher owsflooger in dee oom gay boong kann man makhen?*
Where do they go to? __	Wohin gehen die? *vohin gayhen dee?*
We'd like to go to... ____	Wir möchten nach... *veer moekhten nakh...*
How long is the trip? ___	Wie lange dauert der Ausflug? *vee langer dowert dayr owsflook?*
How long do we _____ stay in...?	Wie lange bleiben wir in...? *vee langer blaiben veer in...?*
Are there any guided ___ tours?	Gibt es Führungen? *gipt ez fyueroongen?*
How much free time ___ will we have there?	Wieviel Freizeit haben wir da? *veefeel fraitsait harben veer dar?*
We want to go hiking____	Wir möchten eine Wanderung machen *veer moekhten ainer vanderoong makhen*

Can we hire a guide?	Können wir einen Führer engagieren?
	koennen veer ainen fuerer engajeeren?
Can I book mountain huts?	Kann ich einen Platz in einer (Berg)hütte reservieren lassen?
	kann ikh ainen plats in ainer (berg)hueter rezerveeren lassen?
What time does... open/close?	Wann öffnet/schliesst (der/die/das)...?
	van oeffnet/shleest (dayr/dee/dass)...?
What days is...open/ closed?	An welchen Tagen ist der/die/das... geöffnet/geschlossen?
	an velkhen targen ist dayr/dee/dass ... geoeffnet/geshlossen?
What's the admission price?	Wieviel kostet der Eintritt?
	veefeel kostet dayr aintrit?
Is there a group discount?	Gibt es Gruppenermässigung?
	gipt es groopen ermayssigoong?
Is there a child discount?	Gibt es Ermässigung für Kinder?
	gipt es ermayssigoong fuer kinder?
Is there a discount for pensioners?	Gibt es Ermässigung für Senioren?
	gipt es ermayssigoong fuer zeneeoren?
Can I take (flash) photos/can I film here?	Darf ich hier (mit Blitzlicht) fotografieren/filmen?
	darf ikh heer (mit blitslikht) foto grafeeren/filmen?
Do you have any postcards of...?	Verkaufen Sie Ansichtskarten von dem/ der...?
	fayrkowfen zee an sikhts karten fon daym/ dayr...?
Do you have an English...?	Haben Sie ein(en)/eine ... auf englisch?
	harben zee ain(en)/ainer ... owf english?
– an English catalogue?	Haben Sie einen Katalog auf englisch?
	harben zee ainen kataloak owf english?
– an English programme?	Haben Sie ein Programm auf englisch?
	harben zee ain program owf english?
– an English brochure?	Haben Sie eine Broschüre auf englisch?
	harben zee ainer broashoorer owf english?

11.2 Going out

● **At the cinema** most films are dubbed (*synchronisiert*). In larger towns and cities as well as art cinemas subtitled versions are often screened, advertised as *Original mit Untertiteln*.

Do you have this _____ week's/month's entertainment guide?	Haben Sie den Veranstaltungskalender von dieser Woche/diesem Monat? *harben zee den fairan shtal toongs kalen der fon deezer vokher/deezem moanart?*
What's on tonight?_____	Was für Veranstaltungen gibt es heute abend? *vass fuer fairan shtal toongen gipt es hoyter arbent?*
We want to go to... _____	Wir möchten in den/ins/in die... *veer moekhten in dayn/ins/in dee...*
Which films are_____ showing?	Welche Filme werden gespielt? *velkher filmer vairden geshpeelt?*
What sort of film is that? _____	Was für ein Film ist das? *vass fuer ain film ist dass?*
rated suitable for _____ the whole family	für jedes Alter *fuer yaydez alter*
rated not suitable for ___ children under 12/16 years	ab 12/16 Jahre(n) *ap tsvoelf/zekh tsayn yahre(n)*
original version _____	Originalfassung *origginaal fassoong*
subtitled_____	untertitelt *oonter teetelt*
dubbed_____	synchronisiert *suen khro nee zeert*
Is it a continuous _____ showing?	Ist es eine durchgehende Vorführung? *ist es ainer doorkh gayhender for fue roong?*

What's on at...?	Was gibt es in...?
	vass gipt es in...?
– the theatre?	Was gibt es im Theater?
	vass gipt es im tayarter?
– the concert hall?	Was gibt es in der Konzerthalle/im Konzertsaal?
	vass gipt es in dayr kontsert haller/im kontsert zarl?
– the opera?	Was gibt es in der Oper?
	vass gipt es in dayr oaper?
Where can I find a good disco around here?	Wo gibt es hier eine gute Disko?
	vo gipt es heer ainer gooter disko?
Is it members only?	Muss man Mitglied sein?
	mooss man mittgleet zain?
Where can I find a good nightclub around here?	Wo gibt es einen guten Nachtklub?
	vo gipt es ainen gooten nakht kloop?
Is it evening wear only?	Ist Abendkleidung Zwang?
	ist arbent klai doong tsvang?
Should I/we dress up?	Ist Abendkleidung erwünscht?
	ist arbent klai doong errvuensht?
What time does the show start?	Wann beginnt die Show?
	vann begint dee shoa?
When's the next soccer match?	Wann ist das nächste Fussballspiel?
	van ist dass nekster foos barl shpeel?
Who's playing?	Wer spielt gegen wen?
	vayr shpeelt gaygen vayn?
I'd like a female/male escort for tonight. Could you arrange that for me?	Ich möchte für heute abend weibliche/männliche Begleitung. Können Sie mir die besorgen?
	ikh moekhter fuer hoyter arbent vai plikher/mennlikher beglaitung. koennen zee meer dee bezorgen?

11.3 Booking tickets

Could you book some__ tickets for us?	Können Sie für uns reservieren? *koennen zee fuer oons rezerveeren?*
We'd like to book... ____ seats/a table...	Wir möchten...Plätze/einen Tisch...reservieren *veer moekhten...pletzer/ainen tish...rezerveeren*
– in the stalls_____	Wir möchten...Plätze/einen Tisch im Parkett reservieren *veer moekhten...pletzer/ainen tish im parkett rezerveeren*

Für welche Vorstellung möchten Sie reservieren?	Which performance do you want to book for?
Welche Plätze bitte?	Where would you like to sit?
Die Vorstellung ist ausverkauft	Everything's sold out
Es gibt nur noch Stehplätze	It's standing room only
Es gibt nur noch Balkonplätze... gibt es noch eine Sondervorstellung	We've only got balcony seats left... there is another special performance
Es gibt nur noch Plätze im Parkett	We've only got stalls seats left
Es gibt nur noch Plätze in den... vorderen Reihen	We've only got seats left in the...front rows
Es gibt nur noch Plätze in den... hinteren Reihen	We've only got seats left in the...back rows
Wieviel Plätze wünschen Sie?	How many seats would you like?
Sie müssen die Karten vor...Uhr abholen	You'll have to pick up the tickets before...o'clock
Ihre Eintrittskarten bitte	Tickets, please
Sie sitzen auf den falschen Plätzen	You're in the wrong seats

– on the balcony_____	Wir möchten...Balkonplätze/einen Tisch auf dem Balkon reservieren
	veer moekhten...balkoanpletzer/ainen tish owf daym balkoan rezerveeren
– box seats _____	Wir möchten...Logenplätze reservieren
	veer moekhten...loagen pletzer rezerveeren
– seats at the front_____	Bitte Plätze vorn
	bitter pletser forn
– seats in the middle ___	Bitte Plätze in der Mitte
	bitter pletser in der mitter
– seats at the back ____	Bitte Plätze hinten
	bitter pletser hinten
Could I book...seats ___ for the...o'clock performance?	Kann ich...Plätze für die Vorstellung von...Uhr reservieren lassen?
	kan ikh...pletser fuer dee for shtel loong fon ...oohr rezerveeren lassen?
Are there any seats left _ for tonight?	Gibt es noch Karten für heute abend?
	gipt es nokh karten fuer hoyter arbent?
How much is a ticket? _	Wieviel kostet eine Karte?
	veefeel kostet ainer karter?
When can I pick the____ tickets up?	Wann kann ich die Karten abholen?
	van kan ikh dee karten aphoalen?
I've got a reservation___	Ich habe reserviert
	ikh harber rezerveert
My name's... _____	Mein Name ist...
	main narmer ist...

12
Sports

12.1 Sporting questions

Where can we... _____ around here?	Wo können wir hier...?
	vo koennen veer heer...?
Is there a... _____ around here?	Gibt es hier in der Nähe ein(en)/eine...?
	gipt es heer in dayr nayher ain(en)/ainer...?
Can I hire a...here? ____	Kann ich hier ein(en)/eine...mieten/leihen?
	kan ikh heer ain(en)/ainer...meeten/laihen?
Can I take...lessons? ___	Kann ich ...Stunden nehmen?
	kan ikh ... shtoonden naymen?
How much is that per __ hour/per day/a turn?	Wieviel kostet das pro Stunde/Tag/Mal?
	veefeel kostet dass pro shtoonder/tark/marl?
Do I need a permit _____ for that?	Braucht man dafür einen Schein/eine Genehmigung?
	browkht man darfuer ainen shain/ainer genay mi goong?
Where can I get _____ the permit?	Wo kann ich die Genehmigung bekommen?
	vo kan ikh dee genay mi goong bekommen?

12.2 By the waterfront

Is it a long way to _____ the sea still?	Ist es noch weit bis ans Meer?
	ist es nokh vait biss ans meer?
Is there a...around here?	Gibt es hier in der Nähe ein... ?
	gipt es heer in dayr nayher ain... ?
-an outdoor/indoor/ _____ public swimming pool	Gibt es hier in der Nähe ein (openair pool) Freibad/(indoor pool) Hallenbad/(public pool) eine Badeanstalt?
	gipt es heer in dayr nayher ain fraibart/ainer hallen bart/ainer barder an shalt/?

– a sandy beach _____	Gibt es hier in der Nähe einen Sandstrand?
	gipt ez heer in dayr nayher ainen sant shtrant?
– a nudist beach _____	Gibt es hier in der Nähe einen Nacktbadestrand?
	gipt ez heer in dayr nayher ainen nakt barder shtrant?
– mooring _____	Gibt es hier in der Nähe einen Anlegeplatz?
	gipt ez heer in dayr nayher ainen anlayger plats?
Are there any rocks here?	Sind hier Felsen?
	zint heer felzen?
When's high/low tide? _	Wann ist Flut/Ebbe?
	van ist floot/ebber?
What's the water temperature?	Welche Temperatur hat das Wasser?
	velkher temperatoor hat dass vasser?
Is it (very) deep here? _	Ist es hier (sehr) tief?
	ist ez heer (zayr) teef?
Can you stand here? _	Kann man hier stehen?
	kan man heer shtayen?
Is it safe to swim here? _	Kann man/(können Kinder) hier ungefährdet schwimmen?
	kan man/(koennen kinder) heer ungefayrdet shvimmen?
Are there any currents? _	Gibt es Strömungen?
	gipt ez shtroe moongen?
Are there any rapids/ waterfalls in this river?	Hat dieser Fluss Stromschnellen/Wasserfälle?
	hat deezer flooss shtrom shnellen/vasser feller?
What does that flag/ buoy mean?	Was bedeutet die Flagge/Boje dort?
	vass bedoytet dee flagger/boayer dort?

139

Achtung! Gefahr!	Angeln verboten	Nur mit Genehmigung
Danger	No fishing	Permits only
Angeln erlaubt	Baden verboten	Surfen verboten
Fishing water	No swimming	No surfing

Is there a life guard ____ on duty here?	Gibt es hier einen Bademeister, der aufpasst?
	gipt es heer ainen barder maister, der owfpasst?
Are dogs allowed ____ here?	Sind hier Hunde erlaubt?
	zint heer hoonder erlowpt?
Is camping on the ____ beach allowed?	Darf man hier am Strand campen?
	darf man heer am shtrant kampen?
Are we allowed to ____ build a fire here?	Darf man hier Feuer machen?
	darf man heer foyer makhen?

12.3 In the snow

Can I take ski lessons __ here?	Kann ich hier Skistunden nehmen?
	kan ikh heer shee shtoonden naymen?
for beginners/ ____ advanced	für Anfänger/(etwas) Fortgeschrittene
	fuer anfenger/(etvass) fortgeshrittenner
How large are the____ groups?	Wie gross sind die Gruppen?
	vee groass zint dee grooppen?
What language are____ the classes in?	In welcher Sprache werden die Stunden gegeben?
	in velkher shprakher verden dee shtoonden gegayben?
I'd like a lift pass, ____ please	Ich möchte einen Ski(lift)pass
	ikh moekhter ainen shee(lift)pass
Must I give you a ____ passport photo?	Muss ich ein Passbild abgeben?
	mooss ikh ain passbilt apgayben?

Where can I have a _____ passport photo taken?	Wo kann ich ein Passbild machen lassen?
	vo kan ikh ain passbilt makhen lassen?
Where are the _____ beginners' slopes?	Wo sind die Skipisten für Anfänger? (jokey): Wo ist der Idiotenhügel?)
	vo zint dee shee pisten fuer anfenger?
	vo ist dayr eedeeoa ten huegel?
Are there any runs for __ cross-country skiing?	Gibt es hier in der Nähe Loipen?
	gipt ez heer in dayr nayher loypen?
Have the cross- _____ country runs been marked?	Sind die Loipen beschildert?
	zint dee loypen beshildert?
Are the...in operation? __	Sind die...geöffnet?
	zint dee...geoeffnet?
– the ski lifts _____	Sind die Skilifte geöffnet?
	zint dee sheelifter geoeffnet?
– the chair lifts _____	Sind die Sessellifte geöffnet?
	zint dee zessel lifter geoeffnet?
Are the slopes usable? _	Sind die Pisten offen?
	zint dee pisten offen?
Are the cross-country __ runs usable?	Sind die Loipen offen?
	zint dee loypen offen?

13

Sickness

13.1 Call (fetch) the doctor

Could you call/fetch a __ doctor quickly, please?
Rufen/holen Sie bitte schnell einen Arzt
roofen/hoalen zee bitter shnell ainen artst

When does the doctor _ have surgery?
Wann hat der Arzt Sprechstunde?
van hat dayr artst shprekh shtoonder?

When can the doctor___ come?
Wann kann der Arzt kommen?
van kan dayr artst kommen?

I'd like to make an _____ appointment to see the doctor
Können Sie für mich einen Termin beim Arzt machen?
koennen zee fuer mikh ainen tairmeen baim artst makhen?

I've got an _____ appointment to see the doctor at...
Ich habe um...Uhr einen Termin beim Arzt
ikh harber oom...ooer ainen tairmeen baim artst

Which doctor/chemist___ has night/weekend duty?
Welcher Arzt/welche Apotheke hat Nachtdienst/Notdienst?
velkher artst/velkher apotayker hat nakht deenst/noat deenst?

13.2 Patient's ailments

I don't feel well _____
Ich fühle mich unwohl
ikh fueler mikh oonvoal

I'm dizzy_____
Mir ist schwindlig
meer ist shvindlikh

– ill_____
Ich bin krank
ikh bin krank

– sick _____
Mir ist schlecht/übel
meer ist shlekht/uebel

I've got a cold_____
Ich bin erkältet
ikh bin erkelltet

It hurts here_____
Ich habe hier Schmerzen
ikh harber heer shmertsen

I've been throwing up __	Ich habe mich übergeben
	ikh harber mikh uebergayben
I've got... _____	Ich habe...Beschwerden
	ikh harber...beshverden
I'm running a_____ temperature of...degrees	Ich habe...(Grad) Fieber *ikh harber...(grart) feeber*
I've been stung by _____ a wasp	Ich bin von einer Wespe gestochen worden
	ikh bin fon ainer vesper geshtokhen vorden
I've been stung by an __ insect	Ein Insekt hat mich gestochen oder gebissen
	ain inzekt hat mikh geshtokhen oader gebissen
I've been bitten by _____ a dog	Mich hat ein Hund gebissen
	mikh hat ain hoont gebissen
I've been stung by _____ a jellyfish	Mich hat eine Qualle gestochen
	mikh hat ainer kvaller geshtokhen
I've been bitten by _____ a snake	Mich hat eine Schlange gebissen
	mikh hat ainer shlanger gebissen
I've been bitten by _____ an animal	Mich hat ein Tier gebissen
	mikh hat ain teer gebissen
I've cut myself _____	Ich habe mich geschnitten
	ikh harber mikh geshnitten
I've burned myself _____	Ich habe mich verbrannt
	ikh harber mikh fayrbrant
I've grazed myself _____	Ich habe eine Hautabschürfung
	ikh harber ainer howt ap shuer foong
I've had a fall _____	Ich bin gestürzt
	ikh bin geshtuertst
I've sprained my ankle _	Ich habe mir den Knöchel verstaucht
	ikh harber meer den knoekhel fairshtowkht
I've come for the _____ morning-after pill	Ich möchte die 'Pille danach' *ikh moekhter dee 'piller darnakh'*

13.3 The consultation

Was für Beschwerden haben Sie? (Wo fehlt's denn?)	What seems to be the problem?
Wie lange haben Sie diese Beschwerden schon?	How long have you had these symptoms?
Haben Sie diese Beschwerden schonfrüher gehabt?	Have you had this trouble before?
Wie hoch ist das Fieber?	How high is your temperature?
Machen Sie sich bitte frei	Get undressed, please
Machen Sie bitte den Oberkörper frei	Strip to the waist, please
Sie können sich dort ausziehen/freimachen	You can undress there
Bitte machen Sie den linken/rechten Arm frei	Roll up your left/right sleeve, please
Legen Sie sich hierauf	Lie down here, please
Tut das weh?/Haben Sie hier Schmerzen?	Does this hurt?
Tief ein- und ausatmen	Breathe deeply
Öffnen Sie den Mund	Open your mouth

Patient's medical history

I'm a diabetic _____ Ich bin zuckerkrank/Diabetiker
ikh bin tsooker krank/deea bayt ikker

I have a heart _____ Ich bin herzkrank/Ich habe ein Herzleiden
condition *ikh bin hairtskrank/ikh harber ain hertslaiden*

I have asthma _____ Ich habe Asthma/Ich bin Asthmatiker
ikh harber astmar/ikh bin astmartikker

I'm allergic to..._____   Ich bin allergisch gegen...
                             ikh bin allairgish gaygen...

Sind Sie gegen irgendetwas allergisch?	Do you have any allergies?
Nehmen Sie Medikamente (ein)?	Are you on any medication?
Haben Sie eine Diät?	Are you on a diet?
Sind Sie schwanger?	Are you pregnant?
Sind Sie gegen Wundstarrkrampf geimpft?	Have you had a tetanus injection?

Es ist nichts Ernstes	It's nothing serious
Sie haben sich den/die/das... gebrochen	Your...is broken
Sie haben sich den/die/das... verstaucht	You've sprained...
Sie haben einen Riss...	You've got (a) torn...
Sie haben eine Entzündung	You've got an inflammation
Sie haben Blinddarmentzündung	You've got appendicitis
Sie haben Bronchitis	You've got bronchitis
Sie haben eine Geschlechtskrankheit	You've got a venereal disease
Sie haben Grippe	You've got the flu
Sie haben einen Herzanfall gehabt	You've had a heart attack
Sie haben eine Infektion (Virus, bakterielle)	You've got an infection (viral, bacterial)
Sie haben Lungenentzündung	You've got pneumonia
Sie haben ein Magengeschwür	You've got an ulcer
Sie haben eine Muskelzerrung	You've pulled a muscle

I'm...months pregnant___	Ich bin...Monate schwanger
	ikh bin...moanarter shvan
I'm on a diet _____	Ich habe eine Diät
	ikh harber ainer deeyayt
I'm on medication/_____	Ich nehme Medikamente/die Pille
the pill	*ikh naymer medee ker menter/dee piller*
I've had a heart attack _	Ich habe schon mal einen Herzanfall
once before	gehabt
	ikh harber shoan mall ainen hertsanfall
	gehapt
I've had a(n)... _____	Ich bin am/an der...operiert
operation	*ikh bin am/an dayr...opereert*

Sie haben eine vaginale Entzündung	You've got a vaginal infection
Sie haben eine Lebensmittelvergiftung/Nahrungs-mittelvergiftung	You've got food poisoning
Sie haben einen Sonnenstich	You've got sunstroke
Sie sind allergisch gegen...	You're allergic to...
Sie sind schwanger	You're pregnant
Ich möchte eine Blut/Harn/Stuhluntersuchung machen lassen	I'd like to have your blood/urine/stools tested
Es muss genäht werden	It needs stitching
Ich schicke Sie zu einem Facharzt/ins Krankenhaus/Hospital	I'm referring you to a specialist/sending you to hospital.
Es müssen Röntgenaufnahmen gemacht werden	You'll need to have some x-rays taken
Setzen Sie sich bitte (wieder) ins Wartezimmer	Could you wait in the waiting room, please?
Sie müssen operiert werden	You'll need an operation

I've been ill recently _____	Ich bin gerade krank gewesen
	ikh bin gerarder krank gevayzen
I've got an ulcer _____	Ich habe ein Magengeschwür
	ikh harber ain margen geshvuer
I've got my period _____	Ich habe meine Periode
	ikh harber mainer peree oader

The diagnosis

Is it contagious? _____	Ist es ansteckend?
	ist ez anshtekkent?
How long do I have to __ stay...?	Wie lange muss ich...bleiben?
	vee langer mooss ikh...blaiben?
– in bed _____	Wie lange muss ich im Bett bleiben?
	vee langer mooss ikh im bett blaiben?
– in hospital_____	Wie lange muss ich im Krankenhaus bleiben?
	vee langer mooss ikh im kranken howz blaiben?
Do I have to go on _____ a special diet?	Muss ich eine Diät einhalten?
	mooss ikh ainer deeyayt ainhalten?
Am I allowed to travel? _	Darf ich reisen?
	darf ikh raizen?
Can I make a new _____ appointment?	Kann ich einen neuen Termin machen?
	kan ikh ainen noyen termeen makhen?
When do I have to _____ come back?	Wann soll ich wiederkommen?
	van zoll ikh veeder kommen?
I'll come back _____ tomorrow	Ich komme morgen wieder
	ikh kommer morgen veeder

Kommen Sie morgen/in ... Tagen wieder	Come back tomorrow/in...days' time

13.4 Medication and prescriptions

Ich verschreibe Ihnen ein Antibiotikum/einen Saft/ein Beruhigungsmittel/Schmerzmittel	I'm prescribing antibiotics/a mixture/a tranquillizer/pain killers
Sie dürfen sich nicht anstrengen/Sie müssen sich schonen	Have lots of rest
Sie dürfen nicht nach draussen	Stay indoors
Sie müssen im Bett bleiben	Stay in bed

alle...Stunden	Kapseln	Spritzen
every...hours	capsules	injections
die Kur beenden	Löffel (Ess-/Tee-)	Tabletten
finish the course	spoonfuls	tablets
dieses Medikament beeinträchtigt die Fahrtüchtigkeit	(tablespoons/ teaspoons)	Tropfen
	...mal täglich	drops
this medication	...times a day	vor jeder Mahlzeit
impairs your driving	nicht zerkauen	before meals
einnehmen	do not chew	während...Tagen
take	nur für äusserliche Anwendung	for...days
einreiben		Zäpfchen
rub on	for external use only	suppository
in Wasser (auf)lösen	Salbe	
dissolve in water	ointment	

How do I take this _____ medicine?	Wie soll ich diese Medikamente einnehmen?
	vee zoll ikh deezer medee kar menter ain naymen?

How many capsules/___ drops/injections/spoon fuls/tablets each time?	Wieviel Kapseln/Tropfen/Spritzen/Löffel/ Tabletten/Zäpfchen pro Mal?
	veefeel kapseln/tropfen/shpritsen/loeffel/ tabletten/tsepfkhen pro marl?
How many times ___ a day?	Wie oft täglich?
	vee oft tayglikh?
I've forgotten my ___ medication. At home I take...	Ich habe meine Medikamente vergessen. Zu hause nehme ich...
	ikh harber mainer medee kar menter fairgessen. tsoo howzer naymer ikh...
Could you make out a__ prescription for me?	Können Sie mir ein Rezept ausstellen?
	koennen zee meer ain retsept ows shtellen?

13.5 At the dentist's

Do you know a good___ dentist?	Können Sie mir einen guten Zahnarzt/Dentisten empfehlen?
	koennen zee meer ainen gooten tsarn artst/denteesten empfaylen?
Could you make a ___ dentist's appointment for me? It's urgent	Können Sie mir einen Termin beim Zahnarzt besorgen? Es eilt
	koennen zee meer ainen termeen baim tsarn artst bezorgen? Ez ailt
Can I come in today, ___ please?	Könnte ich bitte heute noch kommen?
	koennter ikh bitter hoyter nokh kommen?
I have (terrible) ___ toothache	Ich habe (schreckliche) Zahnschmerzen
	ikh harber (shrek likher) tsarn shmertsen
Could you prescribe/___ give me a painkiller?	Können Sie mir ein Schmerzmittel verschreiben/geben?
	koennen zee meer ain shmairts mittel fairshraiben/gayben?
A piece of my tooth/ ___ molar has broken off	Mir ist ein Stück vom Zahn/Backenzahn abgebrochen
	meer ist ain shtuek fom tsarn/bakkentsarn apgebrokhen

My filling's come out ___	Ich habe eine Füllung verloren
	ikh harber ainer fuellung fairloren
I've got a broken _____ crown	Mir ist eine Krone abgebrochen
	meer ist ainer kroner apgebrokhen
I'd like/I don't want a___ local anaesthetic	Ich möchte (nicht) örtlich betäubt werden
	ikh moekhter (nikht) oertlikh betoypt verden
Can you do a _____ makeshift repair job?	Können Sie mir jetzt provisorisch helfen?
	koennen zee meer yetst provee zorish helfen?
I don't want this tooth___ pulled	Ich will nicht, dass dieser Zahn gezogen wird
	ikh vill nikht, dass deezer tsarn getsoagen virt
My dentures are _____ broken. Can you fix them?	Mein Gebiss ist zerbrochen. Können Sie es reparieren?
	main gebiss ist tsayrbrokhen. koennen zee es repareeren?

Welcher Zahn/(Backenzahn) tut weh?	Which tooth hurts?
Sie haben ein(en) Abszess	You've got an abscess
Ich muss eine Nervenbehandlung machen/durchführen	I'll have to do a root canal
Ich betäube Sie örtlich	I'm giving you a local anaesthetic
Ich muss diesen... füllen/ziehen/abschleifen	I'll have to fill/pull/file this tooth
Ich muss bohren	I'll have to drill
Mund auf, bitte	Open wide, please
Mund zu, bitte	Close your mouth, please
Spülen, bitte	Rinse, please
Tut es noch weh?	Does it hurt still?

14.1 Asking for help

Help!	Hilfe!
	hillfer!
Fire!	Feuer!
	foyer!
Police!	Polizei!
	poleetsai!
Quick!	Schnell!
	shnell!
Danger!	Gefahr!
	gefahr!
Watch out!	Achtung!
	akhtoong!
Stop!	Halt!
	halt!
Be careful!	Vorsicht!
	forzikht!
Don't!	Nicht tun!
	nikht toon!
Let go!	Loslassen!
	loaslassen!
Stop that thief!	Haltet den Dieb!
	haltet den deep!
Could you help me, please?	Würden Sie mir bitte helfen?
	vuerden zee meer bitter helfen?
Where's the police station/emergency exit/fire escape?	Wo ist die Polizeiwache/der Notausgang/die Feuertreppe?
	vo ist dee polee tsai vakher/der noat ows gang/dee foyer trepper?
Where's the fire extinguisher?	Wo ist ein Feuerlöscher?
	vo ist ain foyer loesher?
Call the fire brigade!	Rufen Sie die Feuerwehr!
	roofen zee dee foyer vair!

Call the police! _____	Rufen Sie die Polizei (an)
	roofen zee dee poleetsai (an)
Call an ambulance! _____	Rufen Sie einen Krankenwagen/Rettungswagen
	roofen zee ainen krunken vargen/rettoongs vargen
Where's the nearest _____ phone?	Wo gibt's ein Telefon?
	vo gipt's ain telefoan?
Could I use your _____ phone?	Darf ich Ihr Telefon benutzen?
	darf ikh eer telefoan benootsen?
What's the emergency _ number?	Wie lautet die Alarmnummer?
	vee lowtet dee alarm noomer?
What's the number for _ the police?	Wie ist die Telefonnummer der Polizei?
	vee ist dee telefoan noomer dayr poleetsai?

14.2 Loss

I've lost my purse/ _____ wallet	Ich habe mein Portemonnaie/meine Brieftasche verloren
	ikh harber main portmonnay/mainer breeftasher fairloren
I left my...yesterday _____	Ich habe gestern mein(en)/meine... vergessen
	ikh harber gestern main(en)/mainer... fairgessen
I left my...here _____	Ich habe hier mein(en)/meine... liegengelassen/stehengelassen
	ikh harber heer main(en)/mainer...leegen gelassen/shtayen gelassen
Did you find my...? _____	Haben Sie mein(en)/meine...gefunden?
	harben zee main(en)/mainer...gefoonden?
It was right here _____	Er/sie/es stand/lag hier
	er/zee/es shtant/lark heer

It's quite valuable _____ Es ist sehr wertvoll
ez ist zayr vayrtfoll

Where's the lost _____ Wo ist das Fundbüro?
property office? *vo ist dass funt buero?*

14.3 Accidents

There's been an _____ Es ist ein Unfall passiert
accident *ez ist ain unfarl passeert*

Someone's fallen into __ Jemand ist ins Wasser gefallen
the water *yaymant ist ins vasser gefallen*

There's a fire _____ Es brennt
ez brennt

Is anyone hurt? _____ Ist jemand verletzt?
ist yaymant fairletst?

Some people have _____ Es gibt (keine) Verletzte(n)
been/no one's been *ez gipt (kainer) fairletste(n)*
injured

There's someone in ____ Es ist noch jemand im Auto/Zug
the car/train still *ez ist nokh yaymant im owto/tsook*

It's not too bad. Don't __ Es ist nicht so schlimm. Machen Sie sich
worry keine Sorgen
*ez ist nikht zo shlimm. makhen zee zikh
kainer zorgen*

Leave everything the ____ Lassen Sie bitte alles, so wie es ist
way it is, please *lassen zee bitter alles, zo vee ez ist*

I want to talk to the ____ Ich will erst mit der Polizei sprechen
police first *ikh vill airst mit dayr poleetsai shprekhen*

I want to take a _____ Ich will erst ein Foto machen
photo first *ikh vill airst ain foto makhen*

Here's my name _____ Hier sind mein Name und meine Adresse
and address *heer zint main narmer unt mainer adresser*

Could I have your_____ name and address?	Geben Sie mir bitte Ihren Namen und Ihre Adresse
	gayben zee meer bitter eeren narmen unt eerer adresser
Could I see some_____ identification/your insurance papers?	Dürfte ich Ihren Ausweis/Ihre Versicherungspapiere sehen?
	duerfter ikh eeren owsvais/eerer fairzikheroongs papeerer zayhen?
Will you act as a_____ witness?	Wollen Sie Zeuge sein?
	vollen zee tsoyger zain?
I need the details for ___ the insurance	Ich brauche die Angaben für die Versicherung
	ikh browkher dee angarben fuer dee fair zikhe roong
Are you insured? _____	Sind Sie versichert?
	zint zee fairzikhert?
Third party or _____ comprehensive?	Haftpflicht oder Vollkasko-Versicherung?
	haftpflikht oader follkassko-fairzikhe roong?
Could you sign here, ___ please?	Unterschreiben Sie hier bitte
	oonter shraiben zee heer bitter

14.4 Theft

I've been robbed _____	Ich bin bestohlen worden
	ikh bin beshtoalen vorden
My...has been stolen ___	Mein(e) ... ist gestohlen worden
	main(er) ... ist geshtoalen vorden
My car's been _____ broken into	Mein Auto ist aufgebrochen worden
	main owto ist owfgebrokhen vorden

14.5 Missing person

I've lost my child/_____ grandmother	Mein Kind/meine Oma ist verschwunden *main kint/mainer oamar ist fairshvoonden*
Could you help me ____ find him/her?	Würden Sie mir bitte suchen helfen? *vuerden zee meer bitter zookhen helfen?*
Have you seen a _____ small child?	Haben Sie ein kleines Kind gesehen? *harben zee ain klaines kint gezayhen?*
He's/she's...years old __	Er/sie ist...Jahre *er/zee ist...yahrer*
He's/she's got_____ short/long/blond/red/ brown/black/grey/curly/ straight/frizzy hair	Er/sie hat kurzes/langes/blondes/rotes/braunes/ schwarzes/graues/lockiges/glattes/gekrä u seltes Haar *er/zee hat koortses/langes/blondes/roates/ brownes/shvartses/growes/lokigges/glatte s/ gekroyzeltes har*
with a ponytail _____	mit Pferdeschwanz *mit pferder shvants*
with plaits _____	mit Zöpfen *mit tsoepfen*
in a bun _____	mit einem Knoten/Dutt *mit ainem knooten/doott*
He's/she's got_____ blue/brown/green eyes	Die Augen sind blau/braun/grün *dee owgen zint blow/brown/gruen*
He's wearing swimming trunks/mountaineering boots	Er trägt eine Badehose/Wanderschuhe *er traykht ainer barder hoazer/vander shooer*
with/without glasses/ __	mit/ohne Brille *mit/oaner briller*
tall/short_____	gross/klein *groass/klain*
This is a photo of _____ him/her	Hier ist ein Bild von ihm/ihr *heer ist ain bilt fon eem/eer*

He/she must be lost ___ Er/sie hat sich sicher verlaufen
er/zee hat zikh zikher fairlowfen

14.6 The police

An arrest

Ihre Fahrzeugpapiere bitte	Your registration papers, please
Sie sind zu schnell gefahren	You were speeding
Sie parken falsch	You're not allowed to park here
Sie haben kein Geld in die Parkuhr gesteckt	You haven't put money in the meter
Ihr Licht brennt nicht	Your lights aren't working
Sie bekommen eine gebühren-pflichtige Verwarnung/einen Strafzettel von...	You are to receive a fine of/a parking ticket for...
Zahlen Sie sofort?	Do you want to pay on the spot?
Sie müssen sofort bezahlen	You'll have to pay on the spot

I don't speak German __	Ich spreche kein Deutsch
	ikh shprekher kain doytsh
I didn't see the sign ___	Ich habe das Schild nicht gesehen
	ikh harber das shilt nikht gezayhen
I don't understand ___ what it says	Ich verstehe nicht, was da steht
	ikh fairshtayher nikht, vass dar shtayt
I was only doing... ___ kilometres an hour	Ich bin nur...Kilometer pro Stunde gefahren
	ikh bin noor...keelomayter pro shtoonder gefahren
I'll have my car ___ checked	Ich werde mein Auto nachsehen lassen
	ikh verder main owto nakh zayhen lassen

was blinded by _____	Der Gegenverkehr hat mich geblendet
oncoming lights	*dayr gaygen fairkair hat mikh geblendet*

At the police station

Wo ist es passiert?	Where did it happen?
Was haben Sie verloren?	What's missing?
Was ist gestohlen (worden)?	What's been taken?
Ihren Ausweis bitte	Could I see some identification?
Wann ist es passiert?	What time did it happen?
Wer war daran beteiligt?	Who was involved?
Gibt es Zeugen?	Are there any witnesses?
Bitte füllen Sie das aus	Fill this out, please
Hier bitte unterschreiben	Sign here, please
Möchten Sie einen Dolmetscher?	Do you want an interpreter?

I want to report a _____ collision/something missing/rape/missing person	Ich möchte einen Zusammenstoss/einen (things missing)Verlust/eine Vergewaltigung anzeigen/(persons missing) Ich möchte eine Vermisstenanzeige machen
	ikh moekhter ainen tsoo zammen shtoas/ainen fairloost/ainer fair gevalti goong an tsaigen/ikh moekhter ainer fayrmissten antsaiger makhen
Could you make out ___ a report, please?	Würden Sie bitte ein Protokoll aufnehmen?
	vuerden zee bitter ain proatoakoll owfnaymen?
Could I have a copy ___ for the insurance?	Geben Sie mir bitte eine Abschrift für die Versicherung
	gayben zee meer bitter ainer apshrift fuer dee fair zeekhe roong

English	German
I've lost everything_____	Ich habe alles verloren
	ikh harber alles fairloren
All my money is gone,__ I don't know what to do	Mein Geld ist alle, ich bin ratlos
	main gelt ist aller, ikh bin rartloas
Could you please _____ lend me some?	Könnten Sie mir bitte etwas leihen?
	koennten zee meer bitter etvass laihen?
I'd like an interpreter ___	Ich möchte einen Dolmetscher
	ikh moekhter ainen dolmetsher
I'm innocent _____	Ich bin unschuldig
	ikh bin oonshuldikh
I don't know anything __ about it	Ich weiss von nichts
	ikh vaiss fon nikhts
I want to speak to _____ someone from the British consulate	Ich möchte jemanden vom britischen Konsulat sprechen
	ikh moekhter yaymanden fom breetishen konsoolart shprekhen
I need to see someone _ from the British embassy	Ich möchte jemanden von der breetischen Botschaft sprechen
	ikh moekhter yaymunden fon dayr britishen boatshaft shprekhen
I want a lawyer who____ speaks...	Ich will einen Rechtsanwalt, der...spricht
	ikh vill ainen rekhts anvalt, dayr...shprikht

15

Word list and Basic grammar

Word list English – German

● **This word list** is meant to supplement the previous chapters. Nouns are always accompanied by the German definite article in order to indicate whether it is a masculine (*der*), feminine (*die*), or a neuter (*das*), word. In a number of cases, words not contained in this list can be found elsewhere in this book, namely in the lists of the parts of the car, the bicycle and the tent. Many food terms can be found in the German-English list in Section 4.7.

A

about	ungefähr	*oongefayr*
above	über	*ueber*
abroad	das Ausland	*dass owsland*
accident	der Unfall	*dayr oonfarl*
adder	die Natter	*dee natter*
addition	die Addition	*dee adittseeyoan*
address	die Adresse	*dee adresser*
admission	der Eintritt	*dayr aintritt*
admission price	der Eintrittspreis	*dayr aintritts praiss*
advice	der Rat	*dayr rart*
after	nach	*nakh*
afternoon	mittags	*mittargs*
aftershave	die After-shave-Lotion	*dee after-shave loatseeyown*
again	erneut	*ayrnoyt*
against	gegen	*gaygen*
age	das Alter	*dass alter*
Aids	(das) Aids	*(dass) aids*
air conditioning	die Klimaanlage	*dee kleemaranlarger*
air mattress	die Luftmatratze	*dee looft mattratser*
air sickness bag	die Spucktüte	*dee shpook tueter*
aircraft	das Flugzeug	*dass flooktsoyk*
airport	der Flughafen	*dayr flookharfen*
alarm	der Alarm	*dayr alarm*

alarm clock	der Wecker	*dayr vekker*
alcohol	der Alkohol	*dayr alkohol*
allergic	allergisch	*allayrgish*
alone	allein	*allain*
always	immer	*immer*
ambulance	der Rettungswagen	*dayr rettoongs vargen*
amount	der Betrag	*dayr betrarg*
amusement park	der Vergnügungs park	*dayr fayr gnue goongs park*
anchovy	die Anschovis	*dee antshoveez*
and	und	*oont*
angry	böse	*boezer*
animal	das Tier	*dass teer*
ankle	der Knöchel	*dayr knoekhel*
answer	die Antwort	*dee antvort*
ant	die Ameise	*dee armaizer*
antibiotics	das Antibiotikum	*dass antee beeotee kum*
antifreeze	das Frostschutzmittel	*dass frost shoots mittel*
antique	alt/(books) antiquarisch	*alt/anteekvarish*
antiques	die Antiquität	*dee antee kveetayt*
anus	der After	*dayr after*
apartment	das Appartement	*dass appartamong*
aperitif	der Aperitif	*dayr appereeteef*
apologies	die Entschuldigung	*dee ent shooldigoong*
apple	der Apfel	*dayr apfel*
apple juice	der Apfelsaft	*dayr apfelzaft*
apple pie	der Apfelkuchen	*dayr apfel kookhen*
apple sauce	das Apfelmus	*dass apfel moos*
appointment	der Termin	*dayr termeen*
apricot	die Aprikose	*dee apree koazer*
	(Aus.) die Marille	*dee Mariller*
April	der April	*dayr aprill*
Archbishop	der Erzbischof	*dayr airts bishoaf*
architecture	die Architektur	*dee arkhee tektoor*
area	die Umgebung	*dee oom gay boong*
arena	die Manege	*dee manerjer*
arm	der Arm	*dayr arm*

arrange	(sich) verabreden	*(sikh) fayr aprayden*
arrive	ankommen	*ankommen*
arrow	der Pfeil	*dayr pfail*
art	die Kunst	*dee koonst*
artery	die Schlagader	*dee shlarkarder*
artichokes	die Artischocke	*dee artee shokker*
article	der Artikel	*dayr arteekel*
artificial respiration	die künstliche Beatmung	*dee kuenstlikher beart moong*
ashtray	der Aschenbecher	*dayr ashenbekher*
ask	fragen	*fragren*
ask for	bitten um	*bitten oom*
asparagus	der Spargel	*dayr shpargel*
aspirin	das Aspirin	*dass asspireen*
assault	die Verge waltigung	*dee fayr gevaltee goong*
at home	zu Hause	*tsoo howzer*
at the front	vorn	*forn*
at the latest	spätestens	*shpaytestenz*
aubergine	die Aubergine	*dee owberjeener*
August	der August	*dayr owgoost*
automatic	automatisch	*owtow mar teesh*
autumn	der Herbst	*dayr hayrpst*
avalanche	die Lawine	*dee laveener*
awake	wach	*varkh*
awning	das Vordach	*dass fordakh*

B

baby	das Baby	*dass baybee*
baby food	die Babynahrung	*dee baybee nahroong*
babysitter	der Babysitter	*dayr baybee zitter*
back (at the)	hinten	*hinten*
back	der Rücken	*dayr ruekken*
bacon	der Speck	*dayr shpek*
bad	schlecht/schlimm	*shlekht/shlim*
bag	die Tasche	*dee tasher*
bakery	der Bäckerei	*dee bekerai*

balcony	der Balkon	*dayr balkoan*
ball	der Ball	*dayr barl*
ballet	das Ballett	*dass balett*
ballpoint pen	der Kugelschreiber/	*dayr koogel shraiber/*
	der Kuli	*dayr koolee*
banana	die Banane	*dee banarner*
bandage	der Verband	*dayr fayrbant*
bank (river)	das Ufer	*dass oofer*
bank	die Bank	*dee bank*
bank pass	die Scheckkarte	*dee shekkarter*
bar	die Bar	*dee bar*
barbecue	das Barbecue	*dass barbekyu*
basketball (to play)	das Baskettballspiel	*dass basket barl shpeel*
bath	das Bad	*dass bart*
bath attendant	der Bademeister	*dayr barder maister*
bath foam	das Schaumbad	*dass showmbart*
bath towel	das Handtuch/(large)	*dass hanttookh/*
	das Badelaken	*dass barder larken*
bathing cap	die Badekappe	*dee barder kapper*
bathing cubicle	die Badekabine	*dee barder kabeener*
bathing suit	der Badeanzug	*dayr barder antsook*
bathroom	das Badezimmer	*dass barder tsimmer*
battery	die Batterie	*dee batteree*
be in love with	verliebt sein in	*fayrleept zain in*
beach	der Strand	*dayr shtrant*
beans	die Bohnen	*dee boanen*
beautiful	schön/prächtig	*shoen/prekhtikh*
beauty parlour	der Kosmetiksalon	*dayr kozmaytik zalong*
bed	das Bett	*dass bett*
bee	die Biene	*dee beener*
beef	das Rindfleisch	*dass rintflaish*
beer	das Bier	*dass beer*
beetroot	die rote Bete	*dee roater bayter*
begin	anfangen/beginnen	*anfangen/beginnen*
beginner	der Anfänger	*dayr anfenger*
behind	(prep.) hinter/	*hinter/*
	(adj.) hinten	*hinten*

Belgian	der Belgier/	*dayr bellgiyer/*
	die Belgierin	*dee bellgiyerin*
Belgium	Belgien	*bellgiyen*
belt	der Gürtel	*dayr guertel*
berth	der Liegeplatz	*dayr leeger plats*
better	besser	*besser*
bicycle	das Fahrrad	*dass far rart*
bicycle pump	die Luftpumpe	*dee looft poomper*
	(fürs Fahrrad)	*(fuers far rart)*
bicycle repairman	der Fahrradhändler	*dayr farrart hendler*
bikini	der Bikini	*dayr bikeeni*
bill	die Rechnung	*dee rekhnoong*
billiards (to play)	Billard spielen	*billyard shpeelen*
birthday	der Geburtstag	*dayr geboorts tark*
biscuit	der Biskuit/der Keks	*dayr biskveet/keks*
bite (to)	beissen	*baissen*
bitter	bitter	*bitter*
black	schwarz	*shvarts*
bland	geschmacklos	*geshmakkloass*
blanket	die Decke	*dee dekker*
bleach	blondieren	*blondeeren*
blister	die Blase	*dee blarzer*
blond	blond	*blont*
blood	das Blut	*dass bloot*
blood pressure	der Blutdruck	*dayr bloot drook*
blouse	die Bluse	*dee bloozer*
blow dry	föhnen	*foenen*
blue	blau	*blow*
board (on)	an Bord	*an bort*
boat	das Boot	*dass boat*
body	der Körper	*dayr koerper*
body milk	die Bodylotion	*dee body loa tseeoan*
boiled	gekocht	*gekokht*
bonbon	die Praline/das Bonbon	*dee praleener/dass bonbon*
bone	der Knochen	*dayr knokhen*
bonnet	die Motorhaube	*dee moator howber*
book (to)	reservieren	*rezayrveeren*

book	das Buch	*dass bookh*
booked	reserviert	*rezayrveert*
booking office	die Vorverkaufsstelle	*dee for fayrkowfs shteller*
bookshop	die Buchhandlung	*dee bookh hand loong*
border	die Grenze	*dee grentser*
bored (to be)	sich langweilen	*zikh langvailen*
boring	langweilig	*langvailikh*
born	geboren	*geboren*
borrow	ausleihen	*owslaihen*
botanical gardens	der Botanische Garten	*dayr boatarnisher garten*
both	beides	*baidez*
bottle	die Flasche	*dee flasher*
bottle-warmer	der Flaschenwärmer	*dayr flashen vermer*
box	der Karton	*dayr karton*
box	die Loge	*dee loajer*
boy	der Junge	*dayr yoonger*
bra	der BH	*dayr bayhar*
bracelet	das Armband	*dass armbant*
braised	gedünstet/gesotten	*geduenstet/gezotten*
brake	die Bremse	*dee bremzer*
brake fluid	die Bremsflüssigkeit	*dee bremz fluessikh kait*
brake oil	das Bremsöl	*dass bremzoel*
bread	das Brot	*dass broat*
break	(zer-)brechen	*(tsair-)brekhen*
breakfast	das Frühstück	*dass frueshtuek*
breast	die Brust	*dee broost*
bridge	die Brücke	*dee brueker*
briefs	der Schlüpfer	*dayr shluepfer*
bring	(mit-)bringen	*(mit-)bringen*
brochure	die Broschüre	*dee broashuerer*
broken	kaputt	*kapoott*
brother	der Bruder	*dayr brooder*
brown	braun	*brown*
brush	die Bürste	*dee buerster*
Brussels sprouts	der Rosenkohl	*dayr rozenkoal*
bucket	der Eimer	*dayr aimer*
bug	das Ungeziefer	*dass oon getseefer*

building	das Gebäude	*dass geboyder*
buoy	die Boje	*dee boayer*
burglary	der Einbruch	*dayr ainbrookh*
burn	verbrennen	*fair brennen*
burnt	angebrannt	*angebrant*
bus	der (Auto-)Bus	*dayr (owtoa-) booss*
bus station	der Busbahnhof	*dayr booss barnhoaf*
bus stop	die Bushaltestelle	*dee booss halter shteller*
business class	Business Class	*bizniss klarss*
business trip	die Geschäftsreise	*dee geshefts raizer*
busy	lebhaft/geschäftig	*layphaft/gesheftikh*
butane camping gas	das Butangas	*dass bootarn gass*
butcher	der Schlachter/	*dayr shlakhter/*
	der Metzger	*dayr mettsger*
butter	die Butter	*dee bootter*
button	der Knopf	*dayr knopf*
buy	kaufen	*kowfen*
by airmail	per Luftpost	*payr looftpost*

C

cabbage	der Kohl	*dayr koal*
cabin	die Kabine	*dee kabeener*
cake	der Kuchen/	*dayr kukhen/*
	das (Stück) Gebäck	*dass (shtuek) gebeck*
cake	die Torte	*dee torter*
cake shop	die Konditorei	*dee kondeetorai*
call	anrufen	*anroofen*
called (to be)	heissen	*haissen*
camera	die Kamera	*dee kammerar*
camp	campen	*kampen*
camp shop	der Campingladen	*dayr kamping larden*
camp site	der Campingplatz	*dayr kamping plats*
camper	das Wohnmobil	*dass voan moabeel*
campfire	das Lagerfeuer	*dass larger foyer*
camping guide	der Campingführer	*dayr kamping fuerer*

camping permit	die Camping-erlaubnis	*dee kamping ayrlowpniss*
cancel (to)	annullieren	*annooleeren*
candle	die Kerze	*dee kayrtser*
canoe (to)	Kanu fahren	*kanoo faren*
canoe	das Kanu	*dass kanoo*
car	das Auto	*dass owtoa*
car	der Waggon	*dayr vaggorn*
car deck	das Autodeck	*dass owtoa deck*
car documents	die Fahrzeugpapiere	*dee far tsoyk papeerer*
car park (multi-storey)	die Parkgarage	*dee parkgararjer*
car seat	der Kindersitz	*dayr kinderzits*
car trouble	die Panne	*dee panner*
carafe	die Karaffe	*dee karaffer*
caravan	der Wohnwagen	*dayr voan vargen*
cardigan	die Jacke	*dee yakker*
careful	vorsichtig	*forzikhtikh*
carrot	die Karotte	*dee karotter*
carton of cigarettes	die Stange Zigaretten	*dee shtanger tsigaretten*
cascade	der Wasserfall	*dayr vasserfall*
cash desk	die Kasse	*dee kasser*
casino	das Kasino	*dass kasseeno*
cassette	die Cassette	*dee kassetter*
castle	das Schloss	*dass shloss*
cat	die Katze	*dee kattser*
catalogue	der Katalog	*dayr kataloag*
cathedral	die Kathedrale	*dee kattee drarler*
cauliflower	der Blumenkohl (S.Ger.,Aus.) der Karfiol	*dayr bloomen koal dayr karfeeol*
cave	die Höhle	*dee hoehler*
CD	die CD	*dee tsaydee*
celebrate	feiern	*faiern*
cellotape	das Klebeband	*dass klayberbant*
cemetery	der Friedhof	*dayr freethoaf*
centimetre	der/das Zentimeter	*dayr/dass tsen tee mayter*
central heating	die Zentralheizung	*dee tsentrarl hai tsoong*
centre	die Mitte	*dee mitter*

centre	das Zentrum	*dass tsen troom*
chair	der Stuhl	*dayr shtool*
chambermaid	das Zimmermädchen	*dass tsimmer maydkhen*
champagne	der Champagner/Sekt	*dayr shampanyer/zekt*
change (alter)	ändern	*endern*
change (one thing for another)	wechseln	*vekhseln*
change (trains)	umsteigen	*oomshtaigen*
change the baby's nappy	wickeln	*vikkeln*
chapel	die Kapelle	*dee kappeller*
charter flight	der Charterflug	*dayr charter flook*
chat up	jemand anmachen/ sich jemand angeln	*yaymant anmakhen/ zikh yaymant angeln*
check	kontrollieren	*kontrolleeren*
check in	sich anmelden	*zikh anmelden*
cheers	Prost/zum Wohl	*prost/tsoom voal*
cheese (mature, mild)	der Käse(alte, junge)	*dayr kayzer (alter, yoonger)*
chef	der Chef	*dayr shef*
chemist	die Drogerie	*dee drogeree*
cheque	der Scheck	*dayr shek*
cherries	Kirschen	*dee keershen*
chess	das Schachspiel	*dass shakhshpeel*
chewing gum	der/das Kaugummi	*dayr/dass kowgoomee*
chicken	das Huhn/Hühnchen/ Hähnchen	*dass hoon/huenkhen/ haynkhen*
chicory	der Chicorée	*dayr chikoree*
child	das Kind	*dass kint*
child's seat	der Kindersitz	*dayr kinderzits*
chilled	gekühlt	*gekuehlt*
chin	das Kinn	*dass kinn*
chips	Pommes frites	*pomm frits*
chocolate	die Schokolade	*dee shoko larder*
choose	wählen	*vaylen*
chop	das Kotelett	*dass kotlayt*
christian name	der Vorname	*dayr fornarmer*
church	die Kirche	*dee keerkher*

church service	der Gottesdienst	*dayr gottes deenst*
cigar	die Zigarre	*dee tseegarrer*
cigar shop	der Tabakladen	*dayr tarbak larden/*
cigarette	die Zigarette	*dee tseegaretter*
cigarette paper	das Zigarettenpapier	*dass tseegaretten papeer*
ciné camera	die Filmkamera	*dee film kamerar*
circle	der Kreis	*dayr krais*
circus	der Zirkus	*dayr tseerkooss*
city map	der Stadtplan	*dayr shtatplarn*
classical concert	das Klassikkonzert	*dass klasseek kontsert*
clean	saubermachen	*zowber makhen*
clean	sauber	*zowber*
clear	deutlich	*doytlikh*
clearance	der Ausverkauf	*dayr owsfairkowf*
clock	die Uhr	*dee ooer*
closed	geschlossen	*geshlossen*
closed off	gesperrt	*geshpayrrt*
clothes	die Kleider	*dee klaider*
clothes hanger	der Kleiderbügel	*dayr klaider buegel*
clothes peg	die Wäscheklammer	*dee vesher klammer*
clothing (piece of)	das Kleidungsstück	*dass klaidoongs shtook*
clothing	die Kleidung	*dee klaidoong*
coach	der Reisebus	*dayr raizerbooss*
coat	der Mantel	*dayr mantel*
cockroach	der Kakerlak	*dayr karkerlak*
cocoa	der Kakao	*dayr kakow*
cod	der Kabeljau	*dayr karbelyow*
coffee	der Kaffee	*dayr kaffay*
coffee filter	der Kaffeefilter	*dayr kaffay filter*
cognac	der Kognak	*dayr konyak*
cold	kalt	*kalt*
cold (a)	die Erkältung	*dee ayrkeltoong*
cold cuts	der Aufschnitt	*dayr owfshnit*
collarbone	das Schlüsselbein	*dass shluessel bain*
colleague	der Kollege	*dayr kolleger*
collision	der Zusammenstoss	*dayr tsoo zammen shtoas*
cologne	das Eau de toilette	*dass oadetwalet*

colour	die Farbe	*dee farber*
colour pencils	die Buntstifte	*dee boont shtifter*
colour TV	der Farbfernseher	*dayr farp fayrn zayer*
colouring book	das Malbuch	*dass marlbookh*
comb	der Kamm	*dayr kamm*
come	kommen	*kommen*
come back	zurückkommen	*tsooruek kommen*
compartment	das Abteil	*dass aptail*
complaint (physical)	das Leiden	*dass laiden*
complaint	die Beschwerde/	*dee beshverder/*
	die Beanstandung	*dee bean shtan doong*
complaints book	das Beschwerdebuch	*dass beshvayrder bookh*
completely	ganz	*gants*
compliment	das Kompliment	*dass kompleement*
compulsory	verpflichtet	*fayrpflikhtet*
concert	das Konzert	*dass kontsayrt*
concert hall	die Konzerthalle	*dee kontsayrt haller*
concussion	die Gehirn -	*dee geheern ayr*
	erschütterung	*shuete roong*
condensed milk	die Kaffeemilch/	*dee kaffay milkh/*
	die Kondensmilch	*dee kondens milkh*
condom	das Kondom/der	*dass kondoam/dayr*
	Pariser/das Gummi	*pareeser/dass goommee*
congratulate	gratulieren	*gratoo leeren*
connection	die Verbindung	*dee fayr bin doong*
constipation	die Verstopfung	*dee fayr shtop foong*
consulate	das Konsulat	*dass konsoolart*
consultation	die Konsultation	*dee kon sool tat tseeoan*
contact lens	die Kontaktlinse	*dee kontakt linzer*
contact lens solution	das Kontaktlinsen mittel	*dass kontakt linzen mittel*
contagious	ansteckend	*anshtekent*
contraceptive	das Verhütungsmittel	*dass fayr hue toongs mittel*
contraceptive pill	die Verhütungspille	*dee fayr hue toongs piller*
cook (verb)	kochen	*kokhen*
cook	der Koch	*dayr kokh*
copper	das Kupfer	*dass koopfer*
copy	die Kopie	*dee kopee*

corkscrew	der Korkenzieher	*dayr korken tseeher*
corn flour	das Maizena	*dass maitsenar*
corner	die Ecke	*dee ekker*
correct	korrekt	*korrekt*
correspond	korrespondieren	*korrespondeeren*
corridor	der Flur	*dayr flooer*
costume	der Anzug	*dayr antsook*
cot	das Kinderbett	*dass kinderbett*
cotton	die Baumwolle	*dee bowmvoller*
cotton wool	die Watte	*dee vatter*
cough	der Husten	*dayr hoosten*
cough mixture	der Hustensaft	*dayr hoostenzaft*
counter	der Schalter	*dayr shalter*
country	das Land	*dass lant*
country code	die Ländernummer	*dee lender noommer*
courgette	die Zucchini	*dee tsookeenee*
course	(med.) die Kur	*dee koor*
cousin	(m) der Cousin/	*dayr koozeen/*
	(f) die Cousine	*dee koozeener*
crab	die Krabbe	*dee krabber*
cream	die Creme	*dee kraymer*
cream (for cooking)	die Sahne/der Rahm/	*dee zarner/dayr rarm*
credit card	die Kreditkarte	*dee kredeet karter*
crisps	die Chips	*dee chips*
croissant	das Croissant/	*dass krwassan/*
	das Hörnchen	*dass hoernshen*
cross (the road)	überqueren	*ueber kvayren*
crossing	die Überfahrt	*dee ueberfart*
cry	weinen	*vainen*
cubic metre	der/das Kubikmeter	*dayr/dass koobeek mayter*
cucumber	die (Salat)gurke	*dee (zalart)goorker*
cuddly toy	das Kuscheltier	*dass kooshelteer*
cuff links	die Manschetten knöpfe	*dee man shetten knoepfer*
cup	die Tasse	*dee tasser*
	(Aus.) die Schale	*dee sharler*
curly	lockig	*lokikh*
current	die Strömung	*dee shtroemoong*

cushion	das Kissen	*dass kissen*
customary	üblich	*ueblikh*
customs	der Zoll/die Zoll - kontrolle	*dayr tsoll/dee tsol-kontroller*
cut	schneiden	*shnaiden*
cutlery	das Besteck	*dass beshtek*
cycle	fahrradfahren	*far-rart fahren*

D

daily	jeden Tag	*yayden tark*
dairy products	Molkereiprodukte	*molkerai prodookter*
damaged	beschädigt	*beshaydikt*
dance	tanzen	*tantsen*
danger	die Gefahr	*dee gefar*
dangerous	gefährlich	*gefayrlikh*
dark	dunkel	*doonkel*
date	die Verabredung	*dee fayr ap ray doong*
daughter	die Tochter	*dee tokhter*
day	der Tag	*dayr tark*
day before yesterday	vorgestern	*forgestern*
dead	tot	*toat*
decaffeinated	koffeinfrei	*koffayeen frai*
December	der Dezember	*dayr detsember*
deck chair	der Strandstuhl/ Strandkorb	*dayr shtrantshtool/ dayr shtrantkorp*
declare (customs)	verzollen	*fayrtsollen*
deep	tief	*teef*
deepfreeze	einfrieren	*ainfreeren*
degrees	Grad	*grart*
delay	die Verspätung	*dee fayrshpaytoong*
delicious	vorzüglich	*fortsueglikh*
dentist	der Zahnarzt/ der Dentist	*dayr tsarnartst/ der denteest*
dentures	das Kunstgebiss	*dass koonstgebiss*
deodorant	das Deo(dorant)	*dass deo(dorant)*
department	die Abteilung	*dee aptailoong*

department store	das Kaufhaus	*dass kowfhows*
departure	die Abfahrt/(flight)	*dee apfahrt/*
	der Abflug	*dayr apflook*
departure time	die Abfahrtszeit	*dee apfahrts tsait*
depilatory cream	die Enthaarungs creme	*dee ent hahroongs kraymer*
deposit (to)	zur Aufbewahrung (geben)	*tsoor owf bevaroong (gayben)*
deposit	die Kaution	*dee kowtseeoan*
dessert	die Nachspeise	*dee nakhshpaizer*
destination	das (End)ziel	*dass (ent)tseel*
destination (mail)	der Bestimmungsort	*dayr be shtimoongs ort*
develop	entwickeln	*entvikkeln*
diabetic	(m.) der Diabetiker/	*dayr deeearbayteeker/*
	(f.) die Diabetikerin	*dee deeearbayteekerin*
dial	wählen	*vaylen*
diamond	der Diamant	*dayr deeearmant*
diarrhoea	der Durchfall	*dayr doorkhfall*
dictionary	das Wörterbuch	*dass voerter bookh*
diesel	der Diesel	*dayr deezel*
diet	die Diät	*dee deeyayt*
difficulty	die Schwierigkeit	*dee shveerikh kait*
dining room	der Speisesaal	*dayr shpaizerzaal*
dining/buffet car	der Speisewagen	*dayr shpaizer vargen*
dinner (to have)	zu Abend essen	*tsoo arbent essen*
dinner	das Abendessen	*dass arbentessen*
dinner jacket	der Smoking	*dayr smoking*
direction	die Richtung	*dee rikhtoong*
directly	direkt	*deerekt*
dirty	schmierig/schmutzig	*shmeerikh/shmootsikh*
disabled	der/die Behinderte	*dayr/dee behin dayrter*
disco	die Disko	*dee disko*
discount	die Ermässigung/	*dee ermaysi goong/*
	der Nachlass	*dayr nakhlass*
dish	das Gericht	*dass gerikht*
dish of the day	das Tagesgericht	*dass targes gerikht*
disinfectant	das Desinfektions-mittel	*dass dez infektseey oanzmittel*

distance	die Entfernung	dee entfayr noong
distilled water	das destillierte Wasser	dass destileerter vasser
disturb	stören	shtoeren
disturbance	die Störung	dee shtoeroong
dive	tauchen	towkhen
diving	der Tauchsport	dayr towkhshport
diving (deep sea)	das Tiefseetauchen	dass teefzaytowkhen
diving board	das Sprungbrett	dass shproongbret
diving gear	die Taucherausrüstung	dee towkher owsruestoong
divorced	geschieden	gesheeden
DIY-shop	der Heimwerkermarkt	dayr haim vayrker markt
dizzy	schwind(e)lig	shvind(e)likh
do	tun	toon
doctor	der Arzt/(lady)	dayr artst/
	die Ärztin	dee ayrtstin
dog	der Hund	dayr hoont
doll	die Puppe	dee pupper
domestic	das Inland	dass inlant
done (cooked)	gar	gar
door	die Tür	dee tuer
double	Doppel-	doppel-
down	unten	oonten
draught	der Zug	dayr tsook
draughts	das Damespiel	dass darmeshpeel
dream	träumen	troymen
dress	das Kleid	dass klait
dressing gown	der Morgenmantel	dayr morgen mantel
drink	trinken	trinken
drinking water	das Trinkwasser	dass trinkvasser
drive	fahren	faren
driver	der Fahrer	dayr farer
driving licence	der Führerschein	dayr fuerershain
drought	die Trockenheit	dee trokkenhait
dry	trocknen	trokknen
dry	trocken	trokken
dry clean	reinigen	rainigen
dry cleaner's	die Reinigung	dee rainigoong

dry shampoo	das Pudershampoo/	*dass pooder shampoo/*
	das Trockenshampoo	*dass trokken shampoo*
dummy	der Schnuller	*dayr shnooller*
during	während	*vayrent*
during the day	tagsüber	*targsueber*

E

ear	das Ohr	*dass oa-er*
ear, nose and throat	der Hals-, Nasen-,	*dayr halz-, narzen-,*
(ENT) specialist	Ohrenarzt (HNO)	*oarenartst (har enn oh)*
earache	die Ohrenschmerzen	*dee oarenshmairtsen*
eardrops	die Ohrentropfen	*dee oarentropfen*
early	früh	*frueh*
earrings	die Ohrringe	*dee oarringer*
earth	die Erde	*dee erder*
earthenware	die Keramik	*dee kayrarmik*
east	der Osten	*dayr osten*
easy	leicht/(comfortable)	*laikht/*
	bequem	*bekvaym*
eat	essen	*essen*
eczema	das Ekzem	*dass ektsaym*
eel	der Aal	*dayr arl*
egg	das Ei	*dass ai*
elastic band	das Gummi	*dass goomee*
electric	elektrisch	*elektrish*
electricity	der Strom	*dayr shtroam*
embassy	die Botschaft	*dee boatshaft*
emergency brake	die Notbremse	*dee noat bremzer*
emergency exit	der Notausgang	*dayr noat owsgang*
emergency number	die Notrufnummer	*dee noat roof noommer*
emergency phone	die Notrufsäule	*dee noat roof zoyler*
emery board	die Nagelfeile	*dee nargelfailer*
empty	leer	*layr*
engaged	verlobt	*fayrloabt*
(to be married)		
engaged	besetzt	*bezetst*

England	England	*englant*
English	englisch	*english*
Englishman	der Engländer	*dayr englender*
Englishwoman	die Engländerin	*dee englenderin*
enjoy	genießen	*geneessen*
entertainment guide	der Veranstaltungs-kalender	*dayr fayr anshtal toongs kalender*
envelope	der Umschlag	*dayr umshlark*
escort	die Begleitung	*dee beglaitoong*
evening	der Abend	*dayr arbent*
evening wear	die Abendkleidung	*dee arbent klai doong*
event	die Veranstaltung	*dee fair an shtal toong*
every time	jedesmal	*yaydezmarl*
everything	alles	*alless*
everywhere	überall	*ueberarl*
examine	untersuchen	*oonter zookhen*
excavation	die Ausgrabung	*dee owsgrarboong*
excellent	ausgezeichnet	*ows getsaikh net*
exchange	(aus)tauschen	*(ows)towshen*
exchange office	das Wechselbüro	*dass vekhsel buero*
exchange rate	der Wechselkurs	*dayr vekhselkoors*
excursion	der Ausflug	*dayr owsflook*
exhibition	die Ausstellung	*dee owsshteloong*
exit	der Ausgang	*dayr owsgang*
expenses	die Unkosten	*dee oonkosten*
expensive	teuer	*toyer*
explain	erklären	*ayrklayren*
express	der Schnellzug	*dayr shnelltsoog*
external	äusserlich	*oysserlikh*
eye	das Auge	*dass owger*
eyedrops	die Augentropfen	*dee owgentropfen*
eyeshadow	der Lidschatten	*dayr leetshatten*
eye specialist	der Augenarzt	*dayr owgenartst*
eyeliner	der Eyeliner	*dayr ailainer*

face	das Gesicht	*dass gezikht*
factory	die Fabrik	*dee fabreek*
fair	die Kirmes	*dee keermess*
fall	stürzen/fallen	*shtuertsen/fallen*
family	die Familie	*dee fameelier*
famous	berühmt	*beruemt*
far away	weit weg	*vait vek*
farm	der Bauernhof	*dayr bowernhoaf*
farmer	der Bauer	*dayr bower*
farmer's wife	die Bäuerin	*dee boyerin*
fashion	die Mode	*dee moader*
fast	schnell	*shnell*
father	der Vater	*dayr farter*
fault	die Schuld	*dee shoolt*
fax	telefaxen	*teleefaksen*
February	der Februar	*dayr febrooar*
	(Aus.) der Feber	*dayr fayber*
feel	fühlen	*fuelen*
feel like	Lust haben	*loost harben*
fence	der Zaun	*dayr tsown*
ferry	die Fähre	*dee fayrer*
fever	das Fieber	*dass feeber*
fill	füllen	*fuelen*
fill out	ausfüllen	*owsfuellen*
filling	die Füllung	*dee fuelloong*
film	der Film	*dayr film*
filter	der/das Filter	*dayr/dass filter*
find	finden	*finden*
fine	der Strafzettel	*dayr shtrarftsettel*
finger	der Finger	*dayr finger*
fire	das Feuer	*das foyer*
fire brigade	die Feuerwehr	*dee foyer vayr*
fire escape	die Feuertreppe	*dee foyer trepper*
fire extinguisher	der Feuerlöscher	*dayr foyer loesher*
first	erst/erste/erster	*ayrst/ayrster/ayrster*

first aid	die Erste Hilfe	*dee ayrster hilfer*
first class	erster Klasse	*ayrster klasser*
fish (verb)	angeln	*angeln*
fish	der Fisch	*dayr fish*
fishing rod	die Angel	*dee angel*
fit	passen	*passen*
fitness centre	das Fitness-Zentrum	*dass fitness-tsentroom*
fitness training	das Fitness-Training	*dass fitness-trayneeng*
fitting room	die Anprobekabine	*dee an prober kabeener*
fix	flicken	*flikken*
flag	die Fahne/die Flagge	*dee farner/dee flagger*
flash bulb	das Blitzbirnchen	*dass blitz birn khen*
flash cube	der Blitzwürfel	*dayr blitzvuerfel*
flash gun	das Blitzgerät	*dass blitzgerayt*
flat	die Etagenwohnung	*dee etarjen voh noong*
flea market	der Flohmarkt	*dayr flohmarkt*
flight	der Flug	*dayr flook*
flight number	die Flugnummer	*dee flooknoommer*
flood	die Überschwemmung	*dee ueber shwem moong*
floor	der Stock/die Etage	*dayr shtok/dee etarjer*
flounder	die Flunder	*dee floonder*
flour	das Mehl	*dass mayhl*
flu	die Grippe	*dee gripper*
fly (insect)	die Fliege	*dee fleeger*
fly (verb)	fliegen	*fleegen*
fly-over	das Viadukt	*dass fiadookt*
fog	der Nebel	*dayr naybel*
foggy (to be)	neblig sein	*nayblikh zain*
folding caravan	der Faltwagen	*dayr faltvargen*
folkloristic	folkloristisch	*folkloristish*
follow	folgen	*folgen*
food	Lebensmittel	*laybens mittel*
food poisoning	die Lebensmittel-vergiftung	*dee laybenzmittel fairgif toong*
foot	der Fuss	*dayr fooss*
for	vor	*for*
forbidden	verboten	*fairboaten*

forehead	die Stirn	*dee shtirn*
foreign	ausländisch	*owslendish*
forget	vergessen	*fairgessen*
fork	die Gabel	*dee garbel*
form	das Formular	*dass formoolar*
fort	die Festung	*dee festoong*
forward	nachschicken	*nakhshikken*
fountain	der Springbrunnen	*dayr shpring broonnen*
frame	das Gestell	*dass geshtel*
franc	der Franken	*dayr franken*
free	frei	*frai*
free	gratis	*grartis*
free time	die Freizeit	*dee fraitsait*
freeze	gefrieren	*gefreeyeren*
French	französisch	*frantsoezish*
French bread	das Stangenweiss brot/die Baguette	*dass shtangenvaiss broat/dee baguetter*
fresh	frisch	*frish*
Friday	der Freitag	*dayr fraitark*
fried	gebacken	*gebacken*
fried egg	das Spiegelei	*dass shpeegelai*
friend	der Freund	*dayr froynt*
friendly	freundlich	*froyntlikh*
frightened	ängstlich	*enkstlikh*
fruit	das Obst	*dass oapst*
fruit juice	der Obstsaft	*dayr oapstzaft*
frying pan	die (Brat)pfanne	*dee (brart)pfanner*
full	voll	*foll*
fun	das Vergnügen/ der Spass	*dass fergnuegen/ dayr shpass*

G

gallery	die Galerie	*dee galleree-er*
game	das Spiel(chen)	*dass shpeel(khen)*
garage	die Werkstatt	*dee verkshtatt*
garbage bag	der Müllsack	*dayr muelzak*

garden	der Garten	*dayr garten*
gas	das Campinggas	*dass kamping gas*
(propane camping)	(das Propangas)	*(dass proaparn gas)*
gastroenteritis	die Magen- und	*dee margen- oont*
	Darmbeschwerden	*darmbeshvayrden*
gate	das Tor	*dass torr*
gauze	der Verbandmull	*dayr fayrbantmool*
gear	der Gang	*dayr gang*
gel	das Gel	*dass jel*
German	deutsch	*doytsh*
Germany	Deutschland	*doytshlant*
get lost	sich verirren	*zikh fayreeren*
get married	heiraten	*hai-rarten*
get off	aussteigen	*owsshtaigen*
gift	das Geschenk	*dass geshenk*
gilt	vergoldet	*fairgoldet*
ginger	der Ingwer	*dayr ingver*
girl	das Mädchen	*dass maydkhen*
girlfriend	die Freundin	*dee froyndin*
giro cheque	der Postbarscheck	*dayr posst barshek*
giro pass	die Giroscheckkarte	*dee geero shek karter*
glacier	der Gletscher	*dayr gletsher*
glass	das Glas	*dass glas*
glasses (sun)	die Sonnenbrille	*dee zonnen briller*
gliding	das Segelfliegen	*dass zaygel fleegen*
glove	der Handschuh	*dayr hantshoo*
glue	der Klebstoff	*dayr klaypshtoff*
gnat	die Mücke	*dee muekker*
go (on foot)	gehen	*gayhen*
go back	zurückgehen/(car)	*tsueruek gayhen/*
	zurückfahren	*tsueruek faren*
go out	ausgehen	*owsgayhen*
goat's cheese	der Ziegenkäse	*dayr tseegen kayzer*
gold	das Gold	*dass golt*
golf	das Golfspiel	*dass golfshpeel*
golf course	der Golfplatz	*dayr golfplats*
gone	weg	*vek*

good day	guten Tag (Aus. servus) (Sw. Grüezi)	*gooten tark zairvoos gruetsee*
good evening	guten Abend	*gooten arbent*
good morning	guten Morgen	*gooten morgen*
good night	gute Nacht	*gooter nakht*
goodbye	der Abschied	*dayr apsheet*
gram	das Gramm	*dass gramm*
grandchild	das Enkelkind	*dass enkelkint*
grandfather	der Opa	*dayr oapa*
grandmother	die Oma	*dee oamar*
grape juice	der Traubensaft	*dayr trowbenzaft*
grapefruit	die Pampelmuse	*dee pampel moozer*
grapes	die (Wein)trauben	*dee (vain)trowben*
grave	das Grab	*dass grarp*
grease	das Fett	*dass fett*
green	grün	*gruen*
green card	die grüne Karte	*dee gruener karter*
greet	begrüssen	*begruessen*
grey	grau	*grow*
grill	grillen	*grillen*
grilled	geröstet	*geroestet*
grocer	der Kaufmann/ Gemüsehändler	*dayr kowfmann/ gemueser haentler*
ground	der Boden	*dayr boaden*
group	die Gruppe	*dee grupper*
guest house	die Pension	*dee penseeoan*
guide (person/book)	der Führer	*dayr fuehrer*
guided tour	die Führung	*dee fueroong*
gynaecologist	der Frauenarzt	*dayr frowenartst*

H

hair	das Haar	*dass har*
hairbrush	die Haarbürste	*dee harbuerster*
hairdresser	der Damen-, Herren- frisör	*dayr darmen-, hayrren frizoer*

hairpins	die Haarnadeln/ Haarklemmen	*dee harnardeln/ harklemmen*
hairspray	das Haarspray	*dass harspray*
half	halb	*halp*
half	die Hälfte	*dee helfter*
half full	halb voll	*halp foll*
ham (boiled)	der Kochschinken	*dayr kokhshinken*
ham (smoked)	der Räucherschinken	*dayr roykher shinken*
hammer	der Hammer	*dayr hammer*
hand	die Hand	*dee hant*
handbrake	die Handbremse	*dee hantbremzer*
handbag	die Handtasche	*dee hant-tasher*
handkerchief	das Taschentuch	*dass tashentookh*
handmade	handgearbeitet	*hant ge ar bai tet*
happy	froh	*fro*
harbour	der Hafen	*dayr harfen*
hard	hart	*hart*
hat	der Hut	*dayr hoot*
hat	die Mütze	*dee muetser*
hayfever	der Heuschnupfen	*dayr hoyshnoopfen*
hazelnut	die Haselnuss	*dee harzelnooss*
head	der Kopf	*dayr kopf*
headache	die Kopfschmerzen	*dee kopf shmer tsen*
health	die Gesundheit	*dee gezoonthait*
health food shop	das Reformgeschäft	*dass reform gesheft*
hear	hören	*hoeren*
hearing aid	das Hörgerät	*dass hoergerayt*
heart	das Herz	*dass hayrts*
heart patient	der Herzkranke	*dayr hayrts kranker*
heater	die Heizung	*dee haitsoong*
heavy	schwer	*shvayr*
heel	die Ferse	*dee fayrzer*
heel (shoe)	der Absatz	*dayr apzats*
hello	Hallo	*hullo*
helmet	der Helm	*dayr helm*
help	helfen	*helfen*
help	die Hilfe	*dee hilfer*

helping	die Portion	*dee portseeyoan*
herbal tea	der Kräutertee	*dayr kroytertay*
herbs	die Gewürze/(green) die Kräuter	*dee gevuertser/ dee kroyter*
here	hier	*heer*
here you are	(giving sb sth) hier/ (on finding sb) da bist du ja!/(on finding sth) da ist es ja!	*heer/dar bist doo yar/ dar ist ez yar*
herring	der Hering	*dayr hayring*
high	hoch	*hokh*
high tide	die Flut	*dee floot*
highchair	der Kinderstuhl	*dayr kindershtool*
hiking	der Wandersport	*dayr vandershport*
hiking trip	die Wanderung	*dee vanderoong*
hip	die Hüfte	*dee huefter*
hire (for)	zu vermieten	*tsoo fairmeeten*
hire	mieten	*meeten*
hitchhike	per Anhalter fahren/ trampen	*payr anhalter faren/ trampen*
hobby	das Hobby	*dass hobby*
holiday	der Feiertag	*dayr fayertark*
holiday	die Ferien/der Urlaub	*dee fayreeyen/dayr oorlowp*
holiday house	die Ferienwohnung	*dee fayreeyen voanoong*
holiday park	der Bungalowpark	*der bungaloapark*
homesickness	das Heimweh	*dass haimvay*
honest	ehrlich	*ayrlikh*
honey	der Honig	*dayr hoanikh*
horizontal	horizontal	*horeetsontarl*
horrible	scheusslich	*shoyslikh*
horse	das Pferd	*dass pfayrt*
hospital	das Krankenhaus (Aus.,Sw.) das Hospital/Spital	*dass krankenhowz dass hospitarl dass shpitarl*
hospitality	die Gastfreundschaft	*dee gast froynt shaft*
hot (spicy)	pikant	*peekant*

hot-water bottle	die Wärmflasche	*dee vayrm flasher*
hotel	das Hotel	*dass hotel*
hour	die Stunde	*dee shtoonder*
house	das Haus	*dass howz*
household items	die Haushaltsartikel	*dee howz halts artee kel*
Houses of Parliament	das Parlaments-gebäude	*dass parlaments geboyder*
housewife	die Hausfrau	*dee hows frow*
how far?	wie weit?	*vee vait?*
how long?	wie lange?	*vee langer?*
hungry (to be)	hungrig	*hoongrikh*
hurricane	der Orkan	*dayr orkarn*
hurry	die Eile	*dee ailer*
husband	der (Ehe) mann	*dayr (ayher) man*
hut (mountain)	die Berghütte	*dee bairghuetter*
hut	die Hütte	*dee huetter*
hyperventilation	die Hyperventilation	*dee hueper ventee la tseeoan*

I

ice cubes	die Eiswürfel	*dee aiz vuer fell*
ice skating	das Schlittschuhlaufen	*dass shlit shoo lowfen*
icecream	das (Speise)eis	*dass shpaizeraiz*
idea	die Idee	*dee eeday*
identification	der Ausweis	*dayr owsvaiss*
identify	identifizieren	*eedentee fi tsee ren*
ill	krank	*krank*
illness	die Krankheit	*dee krankhait*
imagination	die Vorstellung	*dee forshtelloong*
immediately	sofort	*zofort*
import duty	Einfuhrzölle	*ainfoor tsoeller*
impossible	unmöglich	*oonmoeglikh*
in	in	*in*
in the evening	abends	*arbents*
in the morning	morgens	*morgens*
included	enthalten/einschliesslich	*enthalten/ainshleesslikh*

indicate	zeigen	*tsaigen*
indicator	der Blinker	*dayr blinker*
industrial art	das Kunstgewerbe	*dass koonstgewayrber*
inexpensive	billig	*billikh*
infection	die Virusinfektion,	*dee veeroos infekts*
(viral, bacterial)	die bakterielle	*eeoan, dee bakteereey*
	Infektion	*eller infektseeoan*
inflammation	die Entzündung	*dee ent tsuen doong*
information	die Angaben	*dee angarben*
information	die Auskunft	*dee owskunft*
information office	das Auskunftsbüro	*dass ows kunfts bueroh*
injection	die Spritze	*dee shpritser*
injured	verletzt	*fayrletst*
innocent	unschuldig	*oonshooldikh*
insect	das Insekt	*dass inzekt*
insect bite	der Insektenstich	*dayr inzekten shtikh*
insect repellent	das Mückenöl	*dass muekkenoel*
inside	drin(nen)	*drin(nen)*
insole	die Einlegesohle	*dee ainlaygesohler*
instructions	die Gebrauchs-	*dee gebrowkhs*
	anweisung	*anvai zoong*
insurance	die Versicherung	*dee fayrzikheroong*
intermission	die Pause	*dee powzer*
international	international	*eenter natseeoa narl*
interpreter	der Dolmetscher	*dayr dolmetsher*
intersection	die Kreuzung	*dee kroytsoong*
introduce oneself	sich vorstellen	*sikh forshtellen*
invite	einladen	*ainlarden*
iodine	das Jod	*dass yot*
Ireland	Irland	*eerlant*
Irish	irländisch	*eerlendish*
Irishman	der Ire	*dayr eerer*
Irishwoman	die Irin	*dee eerin*
iron (verb)	bügeln	*byoogelln*
iron	das Bügeleisen	*dass buegell aizen*
ironing board	das Bügelbrett	*dass buegelbrett*
island	die Insel	*dee inzel*

Italian	italienisch	*italeeaynish*
Italy	Italien	*itarlee-en*
itch	das Jucken	*dass yooken*

J

jack	der Wagenheber	*dayr vargen hayber*
jacket	die Jacke	*dee yakker*
jam	die Marmelade	*dee marmelarder*
January	der Januar	*dayr yanooar/*
	(Aus.) der Jenner	*dayr yenner*
jaw	der Kiefer	*dayr keefer*
jellyfish	die Qualle	*dee kvaller*
jeweller	der Juwelier	*dayr yoovayleer*
jewellery	der Schmuck	*dayr shmook*
jog	joggen	*joggen*
joke	der Witz	*dayr vits*
juice	der Saft	*dayr zaft*
July	der Juli	*dayr yoolee*
jumble sale	der Flohmarkt	*dayr flohmarkt*
jump leads	das Startkabel	*dass shtartkarbel*
jumper	der Pullover	*dayr pullover*
June	der Juni	*dayr yooni*

K

key (ignition)	der Zündschlüssel	*dayr tsuent shluessel*
key	der Schlüssel	*dayr shluessel*
kilo	das Kilo	*dass keelo*
kilometre	der Kilometer	*dayr keelo mayter*
king	der König	*dayr koenikh*
kiss (verb)	küssen	*kuessen*
kiss	der Kuss	*dayr kooss*
kitchen	die Küche	*dee kuekher*
knee	das Knie	*dass knee*
knee socks	Kniestrümpfe	*dee knee shtruempfer*
knife	das Messer	*dass messer*

| knit | stricken | *shtrikken* |
| know | wissen | *vissen* |

L

lace	der Schnürsenkel	*dayr shnuerzenkel*
ladies toilet	die Damentoilette	*dee darmen twalet ter*
lake	der See	*dayr zay*
lamp	die Lampe	*dee lamper*
land	landen	*landen*
lane	die Fahrspur	*dee fahrshpoor*
language	die Sprache	*dee shprakher*
large	gross	*groass*
last	letzte	*letster*
late	spät	*shpayt*
later	nachher	*nakh her*
laugh	lachen	*lakhen*
launderette	die Münzwäscherei	*dee muents vesheray*
law	das Recht	*dass rekht*
laxative	das Abführmittel	*dass ap fuer mittel*
leaded	das Super(benzin)	*dass zooper(bentseen)*
leak	das Loch	*dass lokh*
leather	das Leder	*dass layder*
leather goods	Lederwaren	*layder varen*
leave	abfahren/abfliegen	*apfahren/apfleegen*
leek	der Porree/der Lauch	*dayr porray/dayr lowkh*
left	links	*links*
left	nach links	*nakh links*
leg	das Bein	*dass bain*
lemon	die Zitrone	*dee tsitroner*
lend	leihen	*laihen*
lens (wide-angle)	das Weitwinkelobjektiv	*dass vait vinkel obyek teef*
lens	die Linse	*dee linzer*
lentils	die Linsen	*dee linzen*
less	weniger	*vayniger*
lesson	die Stunde	*dee shtoonder*
letter	der Brief	*dayr breef*

lettuce	der Kopfsalat	*dayr kopfzalart*
level crossing	der Bahnübergang	*dayr barn ueber gang*
library	die Bibliothek	*dee beebleeotayk*
lie (tell lie)	lügen	*luegen*
lie	liegen	*leegen*
lift (hitchhike)	die Mitfahr gelegenheit	*dee mit far gelaygenhait*
lift (in building)	der Fahrstuhl/der Aufzug	*dayr farshtool/ der owftsook*
lift (ski)	der (Sessel)lift	*dayr (zessel)lift*
light (not dark)	hell	*hell*
light (not heavy)	leicht	*laikht*
lighter	das Feuerzeug	*dass foyer tsoyk*
lighthouse	der Leuchtturm	*dayr loykht toorm*
lightning	der Blitz	*dayr blits*
like	mögen/(stronger) lieben	*moergen/leeben*
line	die Linie	*dee leenier*
linen	das Leinen	*dass lainen*
lipstick	der Lippenstift	*dayr lippen shtift*
liqueur	der Likör	*dayr leekoer*
liquorice	die Lakritze(n)	*dee lakritzer(n)*
listen	(zu)hören	*(tsoo)hoeren*
literature	die Literatur	*dee literatoor*
litre	der/das Liter	*dayr/dass leeter*
little	wenig	*vaynikh*
little (a)	das bisschen, ein bisschen	*dass bis-shen, ain bis-shen*
live	wohnen	*voanen*
live together	zusammenleben	*tsoo zammen layben*
lobster	der Hummer	*dayr hoommer*
local	örtlich	*oertlikh*
lock	das Schloss	*dass shloss*
locker (luggage)	das Schliessfach (für Gepäck)	*dass shleesfakh (fuer gepek)*
long	lang	*lang*
look	schauen	*showern*
look for	suchen	*zookhen*

look up	aufsuchen	owfzookhen
lorry	der LKW/der Last-wagen	dayr ellkarvay/ dayr lasstvargen
lose	verlieren	fayrleeren
loss	der Verlust	dayr fayrloost
lost	(gen.)weg/(also people) vermisst	vek/fayrmisst
lost	verloren	fayrloren
lost property office	das Fundbüro	dass foontbuero
lotion	die Lotion	dee loatseeoan
loud	laut	lowt
love	sich lieben	zikh leeben
love	die Liebe	dee leeber
low	niedrig	needrikh
low tide	die Ebbe	dee ebber
luck	das Glück	dass gluek
luggage (left)	die Gepäck-aufbewahrung	dee gepek owfbevaroong
luggage	das Gepäck	dass gepek
luggage locker	das Schliessfach	dass shleesfakh
lumps (sugar)	die Zuckerwürfel	dee tsooker wuerfel
lunch	das Mittagessen	dass mittark essen
lungs	die Lungen	dee loongen

M

macaroni	Makkaroni	makaroanee
machine (vending)	der Automat	dayr owtomart
madam	meine Dame	mainer darmer
magazine	die Zeitschrift	dee tsaitshrift
mail	die Post	dee post
make an appointment	einen Termin machen	ainen tairmeen makhen
makeshift	provisorisch	proveezorish
manager	der Verwalter	dayr fayrvalter
mandarin	die Mandarine	dee mandareener
manicure	die Maniküre	dee manee kuerer
map	die (Land)karte	dee (lant)karter

marble	der Marmor	*dayr marmor*
March	der März	*dayr mayrts*
margarine	die Margarine	*dee margareener*
marina	der Yachthafen	*dayr yakht harfen*
market	der Markt	*dayr markt*
marriage	die Ehe	*dee ayher*
married	verheiratet	*fayrhai-rartet*
mass	die Messe	*dee messer*
massage	die Massage	*dee massarjer*
match	der Wettkampf	*dayr vetkampf*
matches	die Streichhölzer	*dee shtraikh hoeltser*
May	der Mai	*dayr mai*
maybe	vielleicht	*feelaikht*
mayonnaise	die Mayonnaise	*dee mayonnayzer*
mayor	der Bürgermeister	*dayr buerger maister*
meal	die Mahlzeit	*dee marltsait*
mean	bedeuten	*bedoyten*
meat	das Fleisch	*dass flaish*
medication	das Heilmittel	*dass hailmittel*
medicine	das Medikament	*dass medee kar ment*
meet	kennenlernen	*kennen layrnen*
melon	die Melone	*dee melowner*
membership	die Mitgliedschaft	*dee mitt gleet shaft*
menstruate	(meine/ihre) Tage haben	*(mainer/eerer) targer harben*
menstruation	die Periode	*dee peereeoader*
menu	das Menü	*dass menue*
menu	die Speisekarte	*dee shpaizer karter*
menu of the day	das Tagesmenü	*dass targez menue*
message	der Bescheid/die Nachricht	*dayr beshait/dee nakhrikht*
metal	das Metall	*dass mettarl*
meter	der/das Taxameter	*dayr/dass taksamayter*
metre	der/das Meter	*dayr/dass mayter*
migraine	die Migräne	*dee meegrayner*
mild (tobacco)	(der) leicht(e) (Tabak)	*(dayr) laikht(er) (tarbak)*
milk	die Milch	*dee milkh*

millimetre	der/das Millimeter	*dayr/dass millimayter*
milometer	der Kilometerzähler	*dayr keelo mayter tsayler*
mince	das Mett/das Hackfleisch	*dass met/ dass hackflaish*
mineral water	das Mineralwasser	*dass minerarl vasser*
minute	die Minute	*dee meenooter*
mirror	der Spiegel	*dayr shpeegell*
miss	vermissen	*fayrmissen*
missing (to be)	fehlen	*faylen*
missing person	vermisste Person	*fayrmisster payrzoan*
mistake	der Fehler/der Irrtum	*dayr fayler/dayr eertoom*
mistaken (to be)	sich irren	*zikh irren*
misunderstanding	das Missverständnis	*dass miss fayr shtant nis*
mocha	der Mokka	*dayr mokker*
modern art	die moderne Kunst	*dee moderner koonst*
molar	der Backenzahn	*dayr bakkentsarn*
moment	der Augenblick	*dayr owgenblik*
moment	der Moment	*dayr moament*
monastery	das Kloster	*dass kloaster*
Monday	der Montag	*dayr moantark*
money	das Geld	*dass gelt*
month	der Monat	*dayr moanart*
moped	das Moped	*dass moaped*
mosque	die Moschee	*dee moshay*
motel	das Motel	*dass moatell*
mother	die Mutter	*dee mooter*
moto-cross	das Moto-Cross	*dass moto-kross*
motorbike	das Motorrad	*dass moatorrart*
motorboat	das Motorboot	*dass moatorboat*
motorway	die Autobahn	*dee owtobarn*
mountain	der Berg	*dayr bayrk*
mountaineering	der Bergsport	*dayr bayrk shporrt*
mouse	die Maus	*dee mows*
mouth	der Mund	*dayr munt*
much/many	viel	*feel*
muscle	der Muskel	*dayr mooskel*
muscle spasms	die Muskelkrämpfe	*dee mooskel krempfer*

museum	das Museum	*dass moozayoom*
mushrooms	die Pilze	*dee piltser*
music	die Musik	*dee moozeek*
musical	das Musical	*dass moozeekall*
mussels	die Muscheln	*dee moosheln*
mustard	der Senf/der Mostrich	*dayr zenf/dayr mosstrikh*

N

nail	der Nagel	*dayr nargel*
nail polish	der Nagellack	*dayr nargellack*
nail polish remover	der Nagellack entferner	*nargel lack entfair ner*
nail scissors	die Nagelschere	*dee nargelsheerer*
naked	nackt	*nakt*
nappy	die Windel	*dee vindel*
National Health Service	die Krankenkasse	*dee kranken kasser*
nationality	die Staatsangehörigkeit	*dee shtarts an gehoerig kait*
natural	natürlich	*natuerlikh*
nature	die Natur	*dee natoor*
naturism	die Freikörperkultur	*dee fray koerper kooltoor*
nauseous	übel	*uebel*
near	bei	*bai*
nearby	in der Nähe	*in dayr nayher*
necessary	nötig/notwendig	*noetikh/noatvendikh*
neck	der Nacken	*dayr nakken*
necklace	die Kette	*dee ketter*
nectarine	die Nektarine	*dee nektareener*
needle	die Nadel	*dee nardel*
negative	das Negativ	*dass negateef*
neighbours	die Nachbarn	*dee nakhbarn*
nephew	der Neffe	*dayr neffer*
never	nie	*nee*
new	neu	*noy*
news	die Nachricht	*dee nakhrikht*
news-stand	der Kiosk	*dayr keeosk*

newspaper	die Zeitung	*dee tsaitoong*
next	nächste(r)	*nekhste(r)*
next to	neben	*nayben*
nice (friendly)/nice (to the eye)	nett/hübsch	*nett/huepsh*
nice (cosy)	gemütlich	*gemuetlikh*
nice (delicious)	lecker	*lekker*
niece	die Nichte	*dee nikhter*
night	die Nacht	*dee nakht*
night (at)	nachts	*nakhts*
night duty	der Nachtdienst	*dayr nakhtdeenst*
nightclub	der Nachtklub	*dayr nakhtkloop*
nightlife	das Nachtleben	*dass nakhtlayben*
no	nein	*nain*
no overtaking	das Überholverbot	*dass ueber hoal fayr boat*
noise	der Lärm	*dayr layrm*
nonstop	nonstop	*nonstop*
no-one	niemand/keiner	*neemant/kainer*
normal	gewöhnlich	*gevoehnlikh*
north	der Norden	*der norden*
normal	normal	*normarl*
north	nördlich	*noerdlikh*
nose	die Nase	*dee narzer*
nose drops	Nasentropfen	*narzen tropfen*
nosebleed	das Nasenbluten	*dass narzen blooten*
notepaper	das Briefpapier	*dass breefpapeer*
nothing	nichts	*nikhts*
November	der November	*dayr november*
nowhere	nirgendwo	*neergentvo*
nude beach	der Nackt(bade)strand	*dayr nakt(barderr) shtrant*
number	die Nummer	*dee noommer*
number (subscriber's)	die Rufnummer	*dee roof noommer*
number plate	das Nummernschild	*dass noommern shilt*
nurse	die (Kranken)schwester	*dee (kranken)shvester*
nutmeg	die Muskatnuss	*dee mooskartnooss*
nuts	die Nüsse	*dee nuesser*

O

October	der Oktober	*dayr oktoaber*
off (food)	verdorben	*fairdorben*
offer	anbieten	*anbeeten*
office	das Büro	*dass buero*
off-licence	der Spirituosen händler	*dayr shpiri too oazen hendler*
oil (diesel)	das Dieselöl	*dass deezeloel*
oil	das Öl	*dass oel*
oil change	der Ölwechsel	*dayr oelvekhsel*
oil level	der Ölstand	*dayr oelshtant*
ointment	die Salbe	*dee zalber*
okay	einverstanden	*ain fayr shtanden*
old	alt	*alt*
olive oil	das Olivenöl	*dass oleevenoel*
olives	die Oliven	*dee oleeven*
omelette	das Omelett	*dass ommlett*
on	auf	*owf*
on the right	rechts	*rekhts*
on the way	unterwegs	*oontervaygs*
oncoming traffic	der Gegenverkehr	*dayr gaygen fayrkayr*
one hundred grams	hundert Gramm	*hoondert gramm*
one-way-traffic	der Einbahnverkehr	*dayr ain barn fayrkayr*
onion	die Zwiebel	*dee tsveebel*
open	öffnen	*oeffnen*
open	offen	*offen*
opera	die Oper	*dee oaper*
operate	operieren	*opereeren*
operator (telephone)	(m) der Telefonist/(f) die Telefonistin	*der telefoanist/ dee telefoanistin*
operetta	die Operette	*dee operetter*
opposite	gegenüber	*gaygenueber*
optician	der Optiker	*dayr optiker*
or	oder	*oader*
orange	die Apfelsine/die Orange	*dee apfel zeener/ dee oranje*

orange juice	der Orangensaft	*dayr oranjenzaft*
order	die Bestellung	*dee beshtelloong*
order (in), tidy	in Ordnung	*in ordnoong*
order	bestellen	*beshtellen*
other	andere/-s	*anderer/-s*
other side	die andere Seite	*dee anderer zaiter*
outside	(dr)aussen/(out wards) raus	*(dr)owssen, rows*
overtake (come alongside)	(overtake)/überholen einholen	*ueber hoalen/ ainhoalen*
oysters	die Austern	*dee owstern*

P

packed lunch	das Lunchpaket	*dass loonch pakayt*
pad (writing)	der Schreibblock (squared, lined)	*dayr shraipblok*
page	die Seite	*dee zaiter*
pain	der Schmerz, (pl.) Schmerzen	*dayr shmayrts, shmayrtsen*
painkiller	das Schmerzmittel	*dass shmayrts mittel*
paint	die Farbe	*dee farber*
painting (art)	die Malerei	*dee marlerai*
painting (object)	das Gemälde	*dass gemelder*
palace	der Palast	*dayr palast*
pan	der Topf	*dayr topf*
pancake	der Eierkuchen/ der Pfannkuchen	*dayr aierkookhen/ dayr pfann kookhen*
pane	die Scheibe	*dee shayber*
panties	der Slip	*dayr slip*
pants	die Unterhose(n)	*dee oonterhoaze(n)*
panty liner	die Slipeinlage	*dee shlip ain larger*
paper	das Papier	*dass papeer*
paper (writing)	das Schreibpapier	*dass shraip papeer*
paprika	der Paprika	*dayr papreeker*
paraffin oil	das Petroleum	*dass petrolayoom*
parasol	der Sonnenschirm	*dayr zonnensheerm*

parcel	das Paket/das Päckchen	dass pakayt/dass pekshen
pardon	die Entschuldigung/die Verzeihung	dee entshool dee goong/dee fayrtsayoong
parents	die Eltern	dee elltern
park	der Park	dayr park
park (car)	parken/(Sw.) parkieren	parken/parkeeren
parking space	der Parkplatz	dayr parkplats
parsley	die Petersilie	dee payterzeelier
part	das (Ersatz)teil	dass (ayrzats)tail
partition	die Trennwand	dee trennwant
partner	der Partner	dayr partner
party	das Fest/die Party	dass fest/dee party
passable	begehbar/(vehicle) befahrbar	begaybar, befarbar
passenger	der Passagier	dayr passajeer
passport	der (Reise)pass	dayr (raizer)parss
passport photo	das Passbild	dass passbilt
patient	der Patient	dayr patseeyent
pavement	der Gehsteig/das Trottoir	dayr gayshtaik/dass trottwar
pay	(be)zahlen	(be)tsarlen
pay the bill	abrechnen	aprekhnen
peach	der Pfirsich	dayr pfeerzikh
peanuts	die Erdnüsse	dee ertnuesser
pear	die Birne	dee beerner
peas	die Erbsen	dee airpsen
pedal	das Pedal	dass pedarl
pedicure	die Fusspflege	dee fusspflayger
pen	der Stift	dayr shtift
pencil	der Bleistift	dayr blaishtift
penis	der Penis	dayr payniss
pension	die Pension	dee ponseeyoan
pepper	der Pfeffer	dayr pfeffer
performance	die Theatervorstellung	dee tayartter for shtelloong
perfume	das Parfüm	dass parfuem

perm (to have a)	eine Dauerwelle machen	*einer dowerveller makhen*
perm	die Dauerwelle	*dee dowerveller*
permit	die Genehmigung/	*dee genay migoong/*
	die Erlaubnis	*dee erlowpniss*
person	die Person	*dee payrzoan*
personal	persönlich	*payrzoenlikh*
petrol	das Benzin	*dass bentseen*
petrol station	die Tankstelle	*dee tank shteller*
pets	die Haustiere	*dee howz teerer*
pharmacy	die Apotheke	*dee appotayker*
phone (tele-)	das Telefon	*dass talayfoan*
phone	telefonieren	*taylayfoaneeren*
phone box	die Telefonzelle	*dee taylayfoan tseller*
phone directory	das Telefonbuch	*dass taylayfoan bookh*
phone number	die Telefonnummer	*dee taylayfown noomer*
photo	das Foto	*dass foto*
photocopier	das Kopiergerät	*dass kopee gerayt*
photocopy	fotokopieren	*foto kopeeren*
photocopy	die Fotokopie	*dee fotokopee*
pick up (an object)	aufheben	*owfhayben*
pick up	(ab)holen	*(ap)hoalen*
picnic	das Picknick	*dass piknik*
pier	die Landungsbrücke	*dee landoongz brueker*
pigeon	die Taube	*dee towber*
pill (contraceptive)	die Pille	*dee piller*
pill (morning-after)	die Pille danach	*dee piller danakh*
pillow	das Kissen	*dass kissen*
pillowcase	der Kissenüberzug	*dayr kissen ueber tsook*
pin	die Stecknadel	*dee shteknardel*
pineapple	die Ananas	*dee anarnass*
pipe	die Pfeife	*dee pfaifer*
pipe tobacco	der Pfeifentabak	*dayr pfaifen tarbak*
pity	schade	*sharder*
place of interest	die Sehenswürdigkeit	*dee zayenz vuerdeekh kait*
plan	der Plan	*dayr plarn*
plant	die Pflanze	*dee pflantser*
plasters	das (Heft)pflaster	*dass (heft)pflaster*

plastic	das Plastik	*dass plastik*
plastic bag	die Tüte	*dee tueter*
plate	der Teller	*dayr teller*
platform	das Gleis	*dass glais*
platform	der Bahnsteig	*dayr barnshtaik*
play (theatre)	das Theaterstück	*dass tayarter shtuek*
play	spielen	*shpeelen*
playground	der Spielplatz	*dayr shpeelplats*
playing cards	die Spielkarten	*dee shpeelkarten*
pleasant	angenehm	*angenaym*
please	bitte	*bitter*
pleasure	das Vergnügen	*dass fairgnuegen*
plum	die Pflaume	*dee pflowmer*
pocketknife	das Taschenmesser	*dass tashen messer*
point	zeigen	*tsaigen*
poison	das Gift	*dass gift*
police	die Polizei	*dee poleetsai*
police station	die Polizeiwache	*dee poleetsai vakher*
policeman	der Polizist	*dayr poleetsist*
pond	der Teich	*dayr taikh*
pony	das Pony	*dass poanee*
pop concert	das Popkonzert	*dass pop kontsert*
population	die Bevölkerung	*dee befoelke roong*
pork	das Schweinefleisch	*dass shvainerflaish*
port	der Port(wein)	*dayr port(vain)*
porter	der Pförtner	*dayr pfoertner*
porter	der Gepäckträger	*dayr gepek trayger*
post code	die Postleitzahl	*dee post lait tsarl*
post office	das Postamt	*dass postamt*
post office (main)	die Hauptpost	*dee howptpost*
postage	das Porto	*dass porto*
postbox	der Briefkasten	*dayr breef kasten*
postcard	die Ansichtskarte/	*dee ansikhts karter/*
	die Postkarte	*dee post karter*
postman	der Briefträger	*dayr breeftrayger*
potato	die Kartoffel	*dee kartoffell*
	(Aus.) die Heurigen	*dee hoyrigen*

200

poultry	das Geflügel	*dass gefluegel*
pound	das Pfund	*dass pfoont*
powdered milk	das Milchpulver	*dass milkhpulver*
power point	der Elektroanschluss	*dayr elektro anshluss*
pram	der Kinderwagen	*dayr kinder vargen*
prawns	die Garnelen	*dee garnaylen*
precious	lieb/teuer	*leep/toyer*
prefer	vorziehen	*fortseehen*
preference	die Vorliebe	*dee forleeber*
pregnant	schwanger/in anderen Umständen	*shvanger/in anderen oomshtenden*
present	vorhanden/(person) anwesend	*forhanden/ anvayzent*
present	das Geschenk	*dass geshenk*
press	drücken	*druekken*
pressure	der Druck	*dayr drook*
price	der Preis	*dayr praiss*
price list	die Preisliste	*dee praisslister*
print	abziehen	*aptseehen*
print	der Abzug	*dayr aptsook*
probably	wahrscheinlich	*varshainlikh*
problem	das Problem	*dass problaym*
profession	der Beruf	*dayr beroof*
programme	das Programm	*dass programm*
pronounce	aussprechen	*owsshprekhen*
pub	die Kneipe	*dee knaiper*
pudding	der Pudding	*dayr pudding*
pull	ziehen	*tseehen*
pull a muscle	sich einen Muskel verzerren	*zikh ainen mooskel fayrtserren*
pure	pur	*poor*
purple	lila	*leelar*
purse	der Geldbeutel	*dayr geltboytel*
purse	das Portemonnaie/die Börse	*dass portmonnay/dee boerzer*
push	schieben/drücken	*sheeben/drueken*
puzzle	das Puzzle	*dass puzzle (pootsel)*

| pyjamas | der Pyjama | *dayr peejarmar* |

Q

quarter	das Viertel	*dass feartell*
quarter of an hour	die Viertelstunde	*dee fear tell shtoonder*
queen	die Königin	*dee koenigin*
question	die Frage	*dee frarger*
quick	schnell	*shnell*
quiet	ruhig	*roohikh*

R

radio	das Radio	*dass rardio*
railway	die (Bundes)bahn	*dee (boondez)barn*
rain	der Regen	*dayr raygen*
rain (verb)	regnen	*raygnen*
raincoat	der Regenmantel	*dayr raygenmantel*
raisins	die Rosinen	*dee rozeenen*
rape	die Vergewaltigung	*dee fair gevalti goong*
rapids	die Stromschnelle(n)	*dee shtroamshneller(n)*
rash	der Ausschlag	*dayr owsshlark*
raspberries	die Himbeeren	*dee himbeeren*
raw	roh	*roa*
raw vegetables	die Rohkost	*dee roakost*
razor blades	die Rasierklingen	*dee razeer klingen*
read	lesen	*layzen*
ready	fertig	*fairtikh*
really	eigentlich	*aigentlikh*
receipt (written)	der Empfangsschein	*dayr empfangs shain*
receipt (till-chit)	der Kassenzettel/die Quittung	*dayr kassentsettel/dee kvittoong*
recipe	das Rezept	*dass retsept*
reclining chair	der Liegestuhl	*dayr leegershtool*
recommend	empfehlen	*empfaylen*
recovery service	die Pannenhilfe	*dee pannen hilfer*
rectangle	das Rechteck	*dass rekhtekk*

...ed	rot	*roat*
...ed wine	der Rotwein	*dayr roatvain*
...eduction	die Ermässigung	*dee ermayssigoong*
...efrigerator	der Kühlschrank	*dayr kuelshrank*
...egion	die Gegend	*dee gaygent*
...egistration	der Kraftfahrzeugschein	*dayr kraft far tsoyk shain*
...elatives	die Verwandten	*dee fayrvanten*
...eliable	zuverlässig	*tsoofayrlessikh*
...eligion	der Glaube(n)/die Religion	*dayr glowber(n)/die religioan*
...ent out	vermieten	*fayrmeeten*
...epair	reparieren	*repareeren*
...epairs	die Reparatur	*dee reparatoor*
...epeat	wiederholen	*veederhoalen*
...eport	die Anzeige	*dee antsaiger*
...esent	übelnehmen	*uebel naymen*
...eset	zurücksetzen	*tsooruek zetsen*
...esponsible	verantwortlich	*fayr antvort likh*
...est	ausruhen	*owsroohen*
...estaurant	das Restaurant	*dass restorant*
...esult	das Ergebnis	*dass ergaypniss*
...retired	pensioniert	*penzeeo neert*
...return (ticket)	die Rückfahrkarte	*dee rueck far karter*
...reverse (vehicle)	rückwärts fahren	*ruekverts faren*
...rheumatism	das Rheuma	*dass roymar*
...rice	der Reis	*dayr raiss*
...ridiculous	unsinnig	*oonzinnikh*
...riding (horseback)	das Reiten	*dass raiten*
...riding school	die Reitschule	*dee raitshooler*
...right	rechts	*rekhts*
...right of way	die Vorfahrt	*dee forfart*
...ripe	reif	*raif*
...risk	das Risiko	*dass reezeeko*
...river	der Fluss	*dayr flooss*
...road	der Weg	*dayr vayk*
...roadway	die Fahrbahn	*dee farbarn*
...roasted	gebraten	*gebrarten*

rock	der Fels(en)	*dayr felz(en)*
roll	das Brötchen	*dass broetshen*
	(S.Ger.,Aus.) die	
	Semmel,	*dee zemmel,*
	der Weck(en)	*dayr vekk(en)*
rolling tobacco	der Shag	*dayr shag*
roof rack	der Gepäckträger	*dayr gepek trayger*
room	das Zimmer	*dass tsimmer*
room number	die Zimmernummer	*dee tsimmer noommer*
room service	der Zimmerservice	*dayr tsimmer zair viss*
rope	das Seil	*dass zail*
rose	die Rose	*dee roazer*
rosé	rosa	*roaza*
roundabout	der Kreisverkehr/der	*dayr krays fayr kayr/*
	Kreisel	*dayr kraizel*
route	die Route	*dee rooter*
rowing boat	das Ruderboot	*dass rooderboat*
rubber	der/das Gummi	*dayr/dass goommee*
rubbish	der Quatsch	*dayr kvatsh*
rucksack	der Rucksack	*dayr rookzak*
rude	unhöflich	*oonhoeflikh*
ruins	die Ruinen	*dee rooeenen*
run (cross-country)	die Langlaufloipe	*dee lang lowf loyper*
run into	treffen	*treffen*

S

sad	traurig	*trowrikh*
safari	die Safari	*dee zafaree*
safe	sicher	*zikher*
safe	das Safe	*dass sayf*
safety pin	die Sicherheitsnadel	*dee zikher haits nardel*
sail	segeln	*zaygeln*
sailing boat	das Segelboot	*dass zaygelboat*
salad	der Salat	*dayr zalart*
salad oil	das Salatöl	*dass zalartoel*
salami	die Salami	*dee zalarmee*

sale	der Ausverkauf	*dayr owsferkowf*
salt	das Salz	*dass zalts*
same	der-/die-/dasselbe	*dayr-/dee-/dasszelber*
sandy beach	der Sandstrand	*dayr zantshtrant*
sanitary pad	die Damenbinde	*dee darmen binder*
sardines	die Sardinen	*dee zardeenen*
satisfied	zufrieden	*tsoofreeden*
Saturday	der Samstag/der Sonnabend	*dayr zamstark/ zonnarbent*
sauce	die Sosse	*dee zoaser*
sauna	die Sauna	*dee zowner*
sausage	die Wurst	*dee voorst*
savoury	herzhaft	*hayrts haft*
say	sagen	*zargen*
scarf	der Schal	*dayr sharl*
scenic walk	der Wanderweg	*dayr vandervayk*
school	die Schule	*dee shooler*
scissors	die Schere	*dee sheerer*
scooter	der Motorroller	*dayr moator roller*
scorpion	der Skorpion	*dayr skorpeeyoan*
Scotland	Schottland	*shottlant*
Scotsman	der Schotte	*dayr shotter*
Scotswoman	die Schottin	*dee shottin*
Scottish	schottish	*shottish*
scrambled eggs	das Rührei	*dass ruehrai*
screw	die Schraube	*dee shrowber*
screwdriver	der Schraubenzieher	*shrowben tseeher*
sculpture	die Bildhauerei	*dee bilt hower rai*
sea	die See/das Meer	*dee zay/dass meer*
seasick	seekrank	*zaykrank*
seat	der Platz	*dayr plats*
seat	der Sitzplatz	*dayr zitsplats*
seat belt	der Gurt	*dayr goort*
seat reservation	die Platzkarte	*dee platskarter*
second	die Sekunde	*dee zekoonder*
second	zweite	*tsvaiter*
second-hand	gebraucht	*gebrowkht*

sedative	das Beruhigungsmittel	*dass berooee goongz mittel*
see (to)	sehen	*zayhen*
see (to) (view)	sich ansehen/besich tigen	*anzayhen/besikh tigen*
self-timer	der Selbstauslöser	*dayr zelpst ows loezer*
send	(ver)schicken	*(fair)shikken*
sentence	der Satz	*dayr zats*
September	der September	*dayr zeptember*
serious	ernst	*ayrnst*
service	die Bedienung	*dee bedeenoong*
serviette	die Serviette	*dee zairveeyeter*
sewing thread	das Nähgarn	*dass naygarn*
shade	der Schatten	*dayr shatten*
shallow	flach	*flakh*
shampoo	das Shampoo	*dass shampoo*
shark	der Hai	*dayr hai*
shave	rasieren	*razeeren*
shaver	der Rasierapparat	*dayr razeer apparart*
shaving brush	der Rasierpinsel	*dayr razeer pinzel*
shaving soap	die Rasierseife	*dee razeer zaifer*
sheet	das Laken	*dass larken*
sherry	der Sherry	*dayr sherry*
shirt	das (Ober)hemd	*dass (oaber)hemt*
shoe	der Schuh	*dayr shoo*
shoe polish	die Schuhcreme	*dee shookraymer*
shoe shop	das Schuhgeschäft	*dass shoogesheft*
shoemaker	der Schuhmacher/ Schuster	*dayr shoomakher/ shooster*
shoes (mountaineering)	die Bergschuhe	*dee bayrk shooer*
shop	einkaufen/einholen	*ainkowfen/ainhoalen*
shop	der Laden	*dayr larden*
shop assistant	die Verkäuferin	*dee fayrkoyferin*
shop window	das Schaufenster	*dass showfenster*
shopping centre	das Einkaufszentrum	*dass ainkowfs tsentroom*
short	kurz	*koorts*
short circuit	der Kurzschluss	*dayr koorts shlooss*

shorts	die kurze Hosen	*dee koortser hoazen*
shoulder	die Schulter	*dee shoolter*
show	die Show/die Schau	*dee shoa/dee show*
shower	die Dusche	*dee doosher*
shutter	der Auslöser	*dayr owsloezer*
side	die Seite	*dee zaiter*
sieve	das Sieb	*dass zeep*
sign	unterschreiben	*oontershraiben*
sign	das Schild	*dass shilt*
signature	die Unterschrift	*dee oonter shrift*
silence	die Stille	*dee shtiller*
silver	das Silber	*dass zilber*
silver-plated	versilbert	*fayrzilbert*
simple	einfach	*ainfakh*
single	unverheiratet/ledig	*oonfayrhai-rartet/laydikh*
single	der Junggeselle/die Junggesellin	*dayr yoong gezeller/dee yoong gezellin*
single	Einzel-	*aintsel-*
single (ticket)	einfach	*ainfakh*
sir	mein Herr	*main hayr*
sister	die Schwester	*dee shvester*
sit	sitzen	*zitsen*
sit down	sich setzen	*zikh zetsen*
size	die Grösse	*dee groersser*
ski	Ski fahren/laufen	*sheefahren/lowfen*
ski boots	Skischuhe	*sheeshooer*
ski goggles	die Skibrille	*dee sheebriller*
ski instructor	der Skilehrer	*dayr sheelairer*
ski lessons/class	die Skistunde(n)	*dee sheeshtoonder(n)*
ski lift	der Skilift	*dayr sheelift*
ski pants	die Skihose	*dee sheehoazer*
ski pass	der Skipass	*dayr sheepass*
ski slope	die Skipiste	*dee sheepister*
ski stick	der Skistock	*dayr sheeshtok*
ski suit	der Skianzug	*dayr sheeantsook*
ski wax	das Skiwachs	*dass sheevakhs*
skiing (cross-country)	der Langlauf	*dayr langlowf*

skimmed	halbfett	*halpfett*
skin	die Haut	*dee howt*
skirt	der Rock	*dayr rock*
skis	die Skier	*dee sheeyer*
skis (cross-country)	die Laufskier	*dee lowf sheeyer*
sleep	schlafen	*shlarfen*
sleeping car	der Schlafwagen	*dayr shlarfvargen*
sleeping pills	die Schlaftabletten	*dee shlarf tabletten*
slide	das Dia	*dass deear*
slip	der Unterrock	*dayr oonterrock*
slip road	die Auffahrt	*dee owffahrt*
slow	langsam	*langzarm*
slow train	der Nahverkehrszug	*dayr narfayrkairs tsook*
small	klein	*klain*
small change	das Wechselgeld	*dass vekhselgelt*
small change	das Kleingeld	*dass klaingelt*
smell	stinken	*shtinken*
smoke	der Rauch	*dayr rowkh*
smoke	rauchen	*rowkhen*
smoked	geräuchert	*geroykhert*
smoking compartment	das Raucherabteil	*dass rowkher aptail*
snake	die Schlange	*dee shlanger*
snorkel	der Schnorchel	*dayr shnorkhel*
snow (verb)	schneien	*shnaien*
snow	der Schnee	*dayr shnay*
snow chains	die Schneekette	*dee shnayketter*
soap	die Seife	*dee zaifer*
soap box	die Seifenschachtel	*dee zaifen shakhtel*
soap powder	das Seifenpulver	*dass zaifen pullfer*
soccer	der Fussball	*dayr fussball*
soccer match	das Fussballspiel	*dass fussball shpeel*
socket	die Steckdose	*dee shtekdoazer*
socks	die Socken	*dee zokken*
soft drink (lemonade)	die Limonade	*dee limonarder*
soft drink	das Erfrischungs-getränk	*dass ayrfrishoongs getrenk*
sole (fish)	die (See)zunge	*dee (zay)tsoonger*

sole	die Sohle	*dee zoaler*
solicitor	der Rechtsanwalt	*dayr rekhts anvalt*
someone	jemand	*yaymant*
sometimes	manchmal	*manshmarl*
somewhere	irgendwo	*eergentvo*
son	der Sohn	*dayr zoan*
soon	bald	*barlt*
sorbet	das Sorbet	*dass sorbay*
sore	das Geschwür	*dass geshvuer*
sore throat	die Halsschmerzen	*dee halz shmayrtsen*
sorry	Entschuldigung/ Verzeihung	*entshool deegoong/ fayrtsayoong*
sort	die Sorte	*dee zorter*
soup	die Suppe	*dee zoopper*
sour	sauer	*zower*
sour cream	der Sauerrahm	*dayr zowerrarm*
source	die Quelle	*dee kveller*
south	der Süden	*dayr zueden*
souvenir	das Andenken/das Souvenir	*dass andenken/dass zooveneer*
spaghetti	die Spaghetti	*dee shpagetti*
spanner (open-ended)	der Gabelschlüssel	*dayr garbel shluessel*
spanner	der Mutternschlüssel	*dayr muttern shluesell*
spare	die Reserve	*dee rezayrver*
spare parts	die Ersatzteile	*dee erzats tailer*
spare tyre	der Reservereifen	*dayr rezayrver raifen*
spare wheel	das Reserverad	*dass rezayrverrart*
speak	sprechen	*shprekhen*
special	besonders	*bezonderz*
specialist	der Spezialist/ der Facharzt	*dayr shpetseealist/dayr fakhartst*
speciality	die Spezialität	*dee shpetseea lee tayt*
speed limit	die Höchst-geschwindigkeit	*dee hoekhst geshvindikh kait*
spell	buchstabieren	*bookh shtarbee ren*
spicy	gewürzt	*gewuertst*
splinter	der Splitter	*dayr shplitter*

spoon	der Löffel	*dayr loeffel*
sport	der Sport	*dayr shport*
sports (to do)	Sport treiben	*shport traiben*
sports centre	die Sporthalle	*dee shporthaller*
spot	der Platz/Ort	*dayr plats/dayr ort*
sprain	verstauchen	*fayrshtowkhen*
spring	der Frühling	*dayr fruehling*
square	der Platz	*dayr plats*
square	quadratisch	*kvadrartish*
square metre	der/das Quadratmeter	*dayr/dass kvadrart mayter*
squash	das Squash	*dass skvash*
stadium	das Stadion	*dass shtadeeon*
stain	der Fleck	*dayr flek*
stain remover	das Fleckenmittel	*dass flekken mittel*
stairs	die Treppe	*dee trepper*
stalls	das Parkett	*dass parkett*
stamp	die Briefmarke	*dee breefmarker*
start	starten/anlassen	*shtarten/anlassen*
station	der Bahnhof	*dayr barnhoaf*
statue	das Standbild/das	*dass shtantbilt/*
	Denkmal	*dass denkmarl*
stay (verb)	bleiben	*blaiben*
stay (verb)	wohnen	*voanen*
stay	der Aufenthalt	*dayr owfenthalt*
steal	stehlen	*shtaylen*
steel (stainless)	der (rostfreie) Stahl	*dayr (rosstfraier) shtarl*
stench	der Gestank	*dayr geshtank*
sting	stechen	*shtekhen*
stitch (med)	nähen	*nayhen*
stock	die Brühe	*dee brueher*
stockings	die Strümpfe	*dee shtruempfer*
stomach	der Magen/der Bauch	*dayr margen/dayr bowkh*
stomach ache	die Magenschmerzen/	*dee margen shmayrtsen/*
	die Bauchschmerzen	*dee bowkh shmayrtsen*
stomach cramps	die Bauchkrämpfe	*dee bowkh krempfer*
stools	der Stuhl(gang)	*dayr shtool(gang)*
stop	halten	*halten*

stop	die Haltestelle	*dee halter shteller*
stopover	die Zwischenlandung	*dee tsvishen landoong*
storm	stürmen	*shtuermen*
storm	der Sturm	*dayr shtoorm*
straight (hair)	glatt(es Haar)	*glatt(ez har)*
straight ahead	geradeaus	*gerarderows*
straw	der Trinkhalm	*dayr trinkhalm*
strawberries	die Erdbeeren	*dee ayrtbeeren*
street	die Strasse	*dee shtrarsser*
street side	die Strassenseite	*dee shtrarssen zaiter*
strike	der Streik	*dayr shtraik*
study	studieren	*shtoodeeren*
subtitled	untertitelt	*oonterteetelt*
succeed	glücken	*gluekken*
sugar	der Zucker	*dayr tsooker*
suit	der Anzug	*dayr antsook*
suitcase	der Koffer	*dayr koffer*
summer	der Sommer	*dayr zommer*
summertime	die Sommerzeit	*dee zommertsait*
sun	die Sonne	*dee zonner*
sun hat	der Sonnenhut	*dayr zonnenhoot*
sunbathe	sich sonnen	*zikh zonnen*
Sunday	der Sonntag	*dayr zonntark*
sunglasses	die Sonnenbrille	*dee zonnenbriller*
sunrise	der Sonnenaufgang	*dayr zonnen owf gang*
sunset	der Sonnenuntergang	*dayr zonnen oonter gang*
sunstroke	der Sonnenstich	*dayr zonnenshtikh*
suntan lotion	die Sonnen(schutz)-creme	*dee zonnen(shoots) kraymer*
suntan oil	das Sonnen(schutz)öl	*dass zonnen(shoots)oel*
supermarket	der Supermarkt	*dayr zooper markt*
surcharge	der Zuschlag	*dayr tsooshlark*
surf	surfen	*zoorfen*
surf board	das Surfbrett	*dass zoorfbrett*
surgery	die Sprechstunde	*dee shprekh shtoonder*
surname	der Nachname	*dayr nakhnarmer*
surprise	die Überraschung	*dee ueber rashoong*

swallow	runterschlucken	*roonter shlooken*
swamp	der Sumpf	*dayr zoompf*
sweat	der Schweiss	*dayr shvaiss*
sweet (a)	das Bonbon	*dass bonbon*
sweet (nice)	lieb	*leep*
sweet (sugary)	süss	*zuess*
sweetcorn	der Mais	*dayr maiss*
sweetener	der Süßstoff	*dayr zuess shtoff*
sweets	Süssigkeiten	*zuessikh kaiten*
swim	schwimmen/baden	*shvimmen/bardern*
swimming pool	das Schwimmbad/	*dass shvimmbart/*
	(spa)die Badeanstalt	*dee barder anshtalt*
swimming trunks	die Badehose	*dee barder hoazer*
swindle	der Betrug	*dayr betrook*
switch	der Schalter	*dayr shalter*
synagogue	die Synagoge	*dee zuena goager*

T

table	der Tisch	*dayr tish*
table tennis	das Tischtennis	*dass tishtennis*
tablet	die Tablette	*dee tabletter*
take	nehmen	*naymen*
take	dauern (time)	*dowern*
take pictures	fotografieren	*foto grafeerren*
talcum powder	der Talkpuder	*dass talkpooder*
talk	reden	*rayden*
tampons	die Tampons	*dee tampons*
tap	der (Wasser)hahn	*dayr (vasser)harn*
tap water	das Leitungswasser	*dass laitoongs vasser*
taste	probieren	*probeeren*
tax free shop	der Taxfree-Shop	*dayr taksfree-shop*
taxi	das Taxi	*dass tarksi*
taxi stand	der Taxistand	*dayr tarksishtant*
tea	der Tee	*dayr tay*
teapot	die Teekanne	*dee taykanner*
teaspoon	der Teelöffel	*dayr tay loeffell*

telegram	das Telegramm	*dass taylaygramm*
telephone (by)	telefonisch	*taylayfoanish*
telephoto lens	das Teleobjektiv	*dass taylay obyek teef*
television	der Fernseher	*dayr fayrnzayer*
telex	das Telex	*dass teleks*
temperature	die Temperatur	*dee temperatoor*
temporary filling	die Notfüllung	*dee noatfueloong*
tender	zart	*tsart*
tennis	das Tennis	*dass tennis*
tennis ball	der Tennisball	*dayr tennisbarl*
tennis court	der Tennisplatz	*dayr tennisplats*
tennis racket	der Tennisschläger	*dayr tennis shlayger*
tent	das Zelt	*dass tselt*
tent peg	der (Zelt)hering	*dayr (tselt)hayring*
terrace	die Terrasse	*dee terasser*
terribly	entsetzlich	*entzetslikh*
thank	danken, sich bedanken	*danken, zikh bedanken*
thank you	vielen Dank	*feelen dank*
thanks	vielen Dank	*feelen dank*
thaw	tauen	*towen*
the day after tomorrow	übermorgen	*ueber morgen*
theatre	das Theater	*dass tayarter*
theft	der Diebstahl	*dayr deepshtarl*
there	da/dort	*da/dort*
thermal bath	das Thermalbad	*dass termarlbart*
thermometer	das Thermometer	*dass termomayter*
thick	dick	*dik*
thief	der Dieb	*dayr deep*
thigh	der Oberschenkel	*dayr oaber shenkel*
thin	dünn/mager	*duenn/marger*
things	die Sachen	*dee zakhen*
think	denken	*denken*
third	das Drittel	*dass drittel*
thirst	der Durst	*dayr doorst*
this afternoon	heute nachmittag	*hoyter nakhmittark*
this evening	heute abend	*hoyter arbent*
this morning	heute morgen	*hoyter morgen*

English	German	Pronunciation
thread	der Faden	*dayr farden*
thread	das Garn	*dass garn*
throat	die Kehle	*dee kayler*
throat lozenges	die Halstabletten	*dee hals tablet ten*
throw up	(sich) erbrechen	*(zikh) ayrbrekhen*
thunderstorm	das Gewitter	*dass gevitter*
Thursday	der Donnerstag	*dayr donnerstark*
ticket (admission)	die (Eintritts)karte	*dee (aintritts)karter*
ticket (travel)	die (Fahr)karte	*dee (far)karter*
ticket	das Ticket	*dass ticket*
tie	die Krawatte	*dee kravatter*
tights	die Strumpfhose	*dee shtroompf hoazer*
time	die Zeit	*dee tsait*
times	mal	*marl*
timetable	der Fahrplan	*dayr farplan*
tin	die Dose/die Büchse	*dee doazer/de buekhser*
tip	das Trinkgeld	*dass trinkgelt*
tissues	Papiertaschentücher	*papeer tashen tuekher*
toast	das Toastbrot	*dass toastbroat*
tobacco	der Tabak	*dayr tabak*
tobacconist's	der Tabakladen	*dayr tabaklarden*
	(Aus.) die (Tabak)	*dayr tabaklarden*
	trafik	*dee (tabak) trafeek*
toboggan	der Schlitten	*dayr shlitten*
today	heute	*hoyter*
toe	der Zeh/die Zehe	*dayr tsay/dee tsayer*
together	zusammen	*tsoozammen*
toilet	die Toilette	*dee twarletter*
toilet	das W.C.	*dass vaytsay*
toilet paper	das Toilettenpapier	*dass twarletten papeer*
toiletries	die Toilettenartikel	*dee twarletten arteekel*
tomato	die Tomate	*dee tomarter*
tomato purée	das Tomatenmark	*dass tomarten mark*
tomato sauce	der Tomatenketchup	*dayr tomarten ketchup*
tomorrow	morgen	*morgen*
tongue	die Zunge	*dee tsoonger*
tonic water	das Tonic	*dass toanik*

tonight	heute nacht	*hoyter nakht*
too much	zuviel	*tsoofeel*
tool	das Werkzeug	*dass vayrktsoyk*
tooth	der Zahn	*dayr tsarn*
toothache	die Zahnschmerzen	*dee tsarnshmayrtsen*
toothbrush	die Zahnbürste	*dee tsarnbuerster*
toothpaste	die Zahnpasta	*dee tsarnpaster*
toothpick	der Zahnstocher	*dayr tsarnshtokher*
top up	nachfüllen	*nakhfuellen*
total	total/insgesamt	*totarl/insgezamt*
tough	zäh	*tsay*
tour	die Rundreise	*dee roontraizer*
tour guide	der Reiseführer	*dayr raizerfuerer*
tourist card	die Touristenkarte	*dee tooristen karter*
tourist class	die Touristenklasse	*dee tooristen klasser*
Tourist Information Office	das Fremdenverkehrs büro	*dass fremden fayrkayrz buero*
tourist menu	das Touristenmenü	*dass tooristen menue*
tow	(ab)schleppen	*(ap)shleppen*
tow cable	das (Ab)schleppseil	*dass (ap)shlepzail*
towel	das Handtuch	*dass hanttookh*
tower	der Turm	*dayr toorm*
town	die Stadt	*dee shtatt*
town hall	das Rathaus	*dass rarthowz*
town walk	der Stadtrundgang	*dayr shtatroontgang*
toy	das Spielzeug	*dass shpeeltsoyk*
traffic	der Verkehr	*dayr fayrkayr*
traffic light	die Verkehrsampel	*dee fayrkayrs ampel*
train	der Zug	*dayr tsook*
train ticket	die Fahr-/Bahnkarte	*dee far-/barnkarter*
train timetable	der Fahrplan	*dayr farplarn*
trainers	die Sportschuhe	*dee shportshooer*
translate	übersetzen	*ueber zetsen*
travel	reisen	*raizen*
travel agent	das Reisebüro	*dass raizer buero*
travel guide	der Reiseführer	*dayr raizerfuerer*
traveller	der/die Reisende	*dayr/dee raizender*

traveller's cheque	der Reisescheck	*dayr raizershek*
treacle/syrup	der Sirup	*dayr zeeroop*
treatment	die Behandlung	*dee behandloong*
triangle	das Dreieck	*dass draiek*
trim	kürzen	*kuertsen*
trip	der Ausflug/die Reise	*dayr owsflook/dee raizer*
trouble	die Beschwerde	*dee beshverder*
trout	die Forelle	*dee foreller*
trunk code	die Vorwahl	*dee forvarl*
try on	anprobieren	*anprobeeren*
tube (inner)	der Schlauch	*dayr shlowkh*
tube	die Tube	*dee toober*
Tuesday	der Dienstag	*dayr deenstark*
tumble drier	der Trockner	*dayr trokner*
tuna	der Thunfisch	*dayr toonfish*
tunnel	der Tunnel	*dayr toonnel*
turn	das Mal	*dass marl*
TV	das T.V./Fernsehen	*dass tayfow/fayrnzayhen*
TV guide	die Rundfunk- und Fernsehzeitschrift	*dee roont foonk- oont fayrn zay tsait shrift*
tweezers	die Pinzette	*dee pintsetter*
tyre	der Reifen	*dayr raifen*
tyre lever	der Reifenheber	*dayr raifen hayber*
tyre pressure	die Reifenspannung	*dee raifen shpannoong*

U

ugly	hässlich	*hesslikh*
umbrella	der Regenschirm	*dayr raygensheerm*
under	unten	*oonten*
underground	die U-Bahn	*dee oo-barn*
underground railway system	das U-Bahnnetz	*dass oo-barnnets*
underground station	die U- Bahnhaltestelle	*dee oo-barn halter shteller*
underpants	die Unterhose	*dee oonterhoazer*
understand	begreifen	*begraifen*
underwear	die Unterwäsche	*dee oontervesher*

undress	sich freimachen/(gen.)	*zikh fraimakhen/*
	sich ausziehen	*zikh owstseehen*
unemployed	arbeitslos	*arbaitsloas*
uneven	ungleichmässig	*oon glaikh mayssig*
university	die Universität	*dee oonee vayrsee tayt*
unleaded	bleifrei	*blaifrai*
up	nach oben	*nakh oben*
urgency	die Eile	*dee ailer*
urgent	dringend	*dringent*
urine	der Harn	*dayr harn*
usually	meistens	*maistens*

V

vacate	räumen	*roymen*
vaccinate	impfen	*impfen*
vagina	die Vagina	*dee vageena*
vaginal infection	die Scheidenentzündung	*dee shaiden ent tsuen doong*
valid	gültig	*gueltik*
valley	das Tal	*dass tarl*
valuable	wertvoll	*vayrtfoll*
van	der Lieferwagen	*dayr leefer vargen*
vanilla	die Vanille	*dee vaniller*
vase	die Vase	*dee varzer*
vaseline	die Vaseline	*dee vasseleener*
veal	das Kalbfleisch	*dass kalpflaish*
vegetable soup	die Gemüsesuppe	*dee gemuezer zupper*
vegetables	das Gemüse	*dass gemuezer*
vegetarian	der Vegetarier	*dayr vegetareeyar*
vein	die Ader	*dee arder*
venereal disease	die Geschlechtskrankheit	*dee geshlekhts krank hait*
via	über	*ueber*
video recorder	der Videorecorder	*dayr video recorder*
video tape	das Videoband	*dass videobant*
view	die Aussicht	*dee owszikht*

village	das Dorf	*dass dorf*
visa	das Visum	*dass veezum*
visit (verb)	besuchen	*bezookhen*
visit	der Besuch	*dayr bezookh*
vitamin	das Vitamin	*dass vitameen*
vitamin tablets	Vitamintabletten	*vitameen tabletten*
volleyball	der Volleyball	*dayr volleyball*
vomit	sich erbrechen	*zikh erbrekhen*

W

wait	warten	*varten*
waiter	der Ober	*dayr oaber*
waiting room	das Wartezimmer	*dass varter tsimmer*
waitress	die Kellnerin/	*dee kelnerin/*
	die Serviererin	*dee zayrveererin*
wake up	wecken	*vekken*
Wales	Wales	*vaylz*
walk	der Spaziergang	*dayr shpatseer gang*
walk (verb)	spazierengehen	*shpatseeren gayhen*
wallet	die Brieftasche	*dee breeftasher*
wardrobe	der Kleiderschrank	*dayr klaider shrank*
warm	warm	*varm*
warn	warnen	*varnen*
warning	die Warnung	*dee varnoong*
warning triangle	das Warndreieck	*dass varn draieck*
wash	waschen	*vashen*
washing	die Wäsche	*dee vesher*
washing line	die Wäscheleine	*dee vesher lainer*
washing machine	die Waschmaschine	*dee vashmasheener*
washing-powder	das Waschmittel	*dass vashmittel*
wasp	die Wespe	*dee vesper*
water	das Wasser	*dass vasser*
water ski	das Wasserski	*dass vassershee*
waterproof	wasserdicht	*vasserdikht*
wave	die Welle	*dee veller*
wave-pool	das Wellenbad	*dass vellenbart*

way	die Weise	*dee vaizer*
way (path)	der Weg	*dayr vayk*
we	wir	*veer*
weak	schwach	*shvakh*
weather	das Wetter	*dass vetter*
weather forecast	der Wetterbericht	*dayr vetter berikht*
wedding	die Hochzeit	*dee hokhtsait*
Wednesday	der Mittwoch	*dayr mitvokh*
week	die Woche	*dee vokher*
weekend	das Wochenende	*dass vokhen ender*
weekend duty	der Notdienst	*dayr noatdeenst*
weekly ticket	die Wochenkarte	*dee vokhen karter*
welcome	willkommen	*villkommen*
well	gut	*goot*
west	der Westen	*dayr vesten*
wet	nass	*nass*
what	was	*vass*
wheel	das Rad	*dass rart*
wheelchair	der Rollstuhl	*dayr rollshtool*
when	wann	*van*
where	wo	*vo*
which	welch-(-e,-er,-es)	*velkh-(-er,-er,-es)*
whipped cream	die Schlagsahne/	*dee shlarkzarner/*
	der Schlagrahm	*der shlarkrarm*
	(Aus.) das Schlagobers	*dass shlarkoberz*
white	weiss	*vaiss*
who	wer	*vayr*
wholemeal	das Vollkorn	*dass follkorn*
wholemeal bread	das Vollkornbrot	*dass follkornbroat*
why	warum	*vahroom*
widow	die Witwe	*dee vitveh*
widower	der Witwer	*dayr vitver*
wife	die Frau	*dee frow*
wind	der Wind	*dayr vint*
windbreak	der Windschutz	*dayr vintshoots*
window	das Fenster	*dass fenster*
windscreen wiper	der Scheibenwischer	*dayr shaiben visher*

wine	der Wein	*dayr vain*
wine card	die Weinkarte	*dee vainkarter*
winter	der Winter	*dayr vinter*
witness	der Zeuge	*dayr tsoyger*
wonderful	herrlich	*hayrlikh*
wood	das Holz	*dass holts*
wool	die Wolle	*dee voller*
word	das Wort	*dass vort*
work	die Arbeit	*dee arbait*
working day	der Arbeits-/der Werktag	*dayr arbaits-/dayr vayrktark*
worn	abgenutzt	*apgenootst*
worried	beunruhigt	*be-oonroo-ikht*
wound	die Wunde	*dee vunder*
wrap (gift)	einpacken	*ainpakken*
wrist	das Handgelenk	*dass hantgelenk*
write	schreiben	*shraiben*
write down	aufschreiben	*owfshraiben*
written	schriftlich	*shriftlikh*
wrong	falsch/verkehrt	*falsh/fayrkayrt*

Y

yacht	die Yacht	*dee yakht*
year	das Jahr	*dass yahr*
yellow	gelb	*gelp*
yes	ja	*yar*
yesterday	gestern	*gestern*
yoghurt	der/(Aus.) das Joghurt	*dayr yoghoort*
you (polite)	Sie	*zee*
you too	gleichfalls	*glaikhfals*
youth hostel	die Jugendherberge	*dee yoogent hayr bayrger*

Z

zebra crossing	der Zebrastreifen	*dayr tsebra shtraifen*
zip	der Reissverschluss	*dayr raiss fayr shlooss*
zoo	der Zoo	*dayr tsoo*

1 Nouns

German nouns are divided into three types, known as genders: masculine, feminine, and neuter. German also has a system of cases for its nouns, four in number, and referred to in English as Nominative (for the subject), Accusative (for the object), Genitive (the possessive case), and Dative (the *to* or *for* case).

2 Definite article (the)

	Masculine	Feminine	Neuter
Nominative	**der**	**die**	**das**
Accusative	**den**	**die**	**das**
Genitive	**des**	**der**	**des**
Dative	**dem**	**der**	**dem**

The plural is the same for all:

Nominative	**die**
Accusative	**die**
Genitive	**der**
Dative	**den**

3 Indefinite article (a or an)

	Masculine	Feminine	Neuter
Nominative	**ein**	**eine**	**ein**
Accusative	**einen**	**eine**	**ein**
Genitive	**eines**	**einer**	**eines**
Dative	**einem**	**einer**	**einem**

Note that when masculine and neuter nouns are in the possessive (genitive) case, they have an s at the end, not totally unlike English; **der Hund des Mannes** (the man's dog).

4 Plurals

Nouns can be rather erratic. There are a few basic principles: Nouns ending in **-keit** and **-heit** and **-ung** add the letters **-en** to form the plural.

Neuheit (novelties) becomes **Neuheiten** (novelties); **Sehenswürdigkeit** (something worth seeing, tourist attraction) becomes **Sehenswürdigkeiten** (tourist attractions); **Hoffnung** (hope) becomes **Hoffnungen** (hopes). Also, as a general rule, if a word ends in an **-e**, assume you can make the plural by adding an n; **Witwe** (widow) becomes **Witwen** (widows). In the case of masculine and neuter nouns making the plural not infrequently involves making a change in the vowels within the word as well as adding an ending. Try adding the sound **-e** or **er** to the singular form, and you should be able to put the meaning across. In the plural form of the Dative case, all nouns add an **-n**. **Berg** (mountain) is a masculine noun (**der Berg**), and becomes **Berge** in the plural (mountains); on the mountains becomes **auf den Bergen**.

5 Adjectives

Adjectives come in front of the noun. There is an arrangement for making the adjective agree with the noun if it is used without any article (no the or a), which is basically like **der**, **die**, **das**; Black thing, for example, is **schwarzes Ding**, pretty woman is **schöne Frau**, big dog is "**grosser Hund**". If we place an article before the adjective, things are easier; the black thing is **das schwarze Ding**, the pretty woman is **die schöne Frau**, the big dog is **der grosse Hund**. Of the black thing; **des schwarzen Dings**. Of the pretty woman; **der schönen Frau**. Of the big dog; **des grossen Hunds**. (You may also hear **Dinges** and **Hundes**.)

6 Adverbs

Adverbs are essentially the same in German as adjectives; in other words, he does it well is **er tut es gut** (*err toot ez goot*), which means he does it good. Know one and you know the other.

7 Pronouns

	First (I)	Second (you)	Third (he)	(she)	(it)
Nominative	**ich**	**Sie**	**er**	**sie**	**es**
Accusative	**mich**	**Sie**	**ihn**	**sie**	**es**
Dative	**mir**	**Ihnen**	**ihm**	**ihr**	**ihm**

The forms for the plural, they, are **sie, sie, ihnen**. Accordingly, he sees me becomes **er sieht mich**; she sees him: **sie sieht ihn**. I see t: **ich sehe es**. The dative case is the case which occurs mostly if prepositions are involved (with, by, from, for example).

There is also a form for you which is used for close friends, talking to very small children, and animals; this is **Du**, and should be avoided unless you are really sure of your ground. There is a plural form of this, **ihr**. The usual word for you is **Sie** (pronounced *zee*), and when written always has a capital letter for its forms, to distinguish it from the forms for they.

8 Verbs

German verbs, like English verbs, come in two kinds, traditionally referred to as strong and weak. Weak verbs are the regular ones, and are easy; strong verbs are irregular, and can really only be learnt. An example of a weak verb in English is to walk; I walk, I walked, I have walked. An example of a strong verb is to swim; I swim, I swam, I have swum. The weak verbs make their forms which indicate action in the past in a regular way, too: I was loving is **ich liebte**; he was loving **er liebte**; we/you/they were loving: **Wir/Sie/sie liebten**. The strong verbs change the vowel in the main part of the verb: **ich schwimme** becomes **ich schwamm** (I swam).

A German weak verb looks like this:

Lieben,	To love
ich liebe	I love (also doubles up for I am loving, I do love)
(Du liebst)	(you love; this is the very friendly form)
er/sie/es liebt	he/she/it loves
wir lieben	we love
Sie lieben	you love
sie lieben	they love

The other difference between weak and strong verbs occurs in the past participle. Weak verbs are regular in their past participles; add the letters **ge-** to the front, and replace the **-en** at the end of the verb by a **-t**. **Lieben** (to love) gives us a past participle **gelebt** (loved);

spielen (to play) gives **gespielt** (played), and so on.
Strong verbs do not make this change; e.g. **schwimmen** gives us **geschwommen** (**swum**), sehen (to see) gives us **gesehen**.

A quick look at the verbs "to have" and "to be":

Haben	To have
ich habe	I have
(Du hast)	(you have; very friendly form)
er/sie/es hat	he/she/it has
wir/Sie/sie haben	we/you/they have
Sein	To be
ich bin	I am
(Du bist)	(you are; very friendly form)
er/sie/es ist	he/she/it has
wir/Sie/sie sind	we/you/they are

In principle, the past form I have (done something) is created by using the relevant part of **haben** for verbs which have an object (I have seen him: **ich habe ihn gesehen**; I have done it: **ich habe es getan**), and the relevant parts of sein for verbs which do not have an object (I have swum: **ich bin geschwommen**; I have come: **ich bin gekommen**; I have flown: **Ich bin geflogen**). Bear in mind that, in the past form using have, the past participle comes at the end of the sentence.

9 Prepositions

in means in or into
auf means on or onto
mit means with
zu means to
for means for
bei means with or in the vicinity of (but rarely by)
von means of or from

Most prepositions are associated with the dative case, although some are found with the accusative e.g. **in der Stadt**: IN the town, **in die Stadt**: INTO the town.